UNITING MISSISSIPPI

UNITING MISSISSIPPI

Democracy and Leadership in the South

Eric Thomas Weber

Foreword by Governor William F. Winter

To Jackie,

thank you for your example

& inspiration!

Sincerely,

2/3/17

Eric Weber

University Press of Mississippi   *Jackson*

www.upress.state.ms.us

The University Press of Mississippi is a member
of the Association of American University Presses.

First printing 2015

∞

Library of Congress Cataloging-in-Publication Data
Weber, Eric Thomas.
  Uniting Mississippi : democracy and leadership in the South / Eric
Thomas Weber ; foreword by Governor William Winter.
    pages cm
  Includes bibliographical references and index.
  ISBN 978-1-4968-0331-3 (cloth : alk. paper) — ISBN 978-1-4968-0349-
8 (pbk. : alk. paper) — ISBN 978-1-4968-0332-0 (ebook) 1. Poor—Mis-
sissippi. 2. Education—Mississippi. 3. Political leadership—Missis-
sippi. 4. Democracy—Mississippi. I. Title.
  HC107.M73P64 2015
  320.609762—dc23

                          2015005237

British Library Cataloging-in-Publication Data available

TO JOANNA HENDERSON,

whose wisdom opened my eyes and whose kindness
helped my family through our most difficult time.

We'll have to find a greater title for [larger cities] because each of them is a great many cities, not *a* city. . . . At any rate, each of them consists of two cities at war with one another, that of the poor and that of the rich, and each of these contains a great many.—Plato, *Republic*, Book IV

Is there any greater evil we can mention for a city than that which tears it apart and makes it many instead of one? Or any greater good than that which binds it together and makes it one?—Plato, *Republic*, Book V

To understand the world, you have to understand a place like Mississippi.—William Faulkner, attributed[1]

The past is never dead. It's not even past.
—William Faulkner, *Requiem for a Nun*

CONTENTS

FOREWORD

By the Honorable Governor William F. Winter

I have spent many hours in the more than ninety years that I
have been privileged to live in my native state of Mississippi
trying to figure out just what have been the elements that
have set it apart in so many ways and that have contributed
to our state's difficulties over the years. This volume comes
about as close as anything that I have read to defining those
factors that, for better or worse, have marked and shaped
our existence.

We must begin by recognizing that we are a state of incredible paradoxes, many of which continue to perplex us.
For example this has been a place where we have prided ourselves on the value that we attach to personal relationships
and to being good neighbors. Yet we have a disproportion-
ately large number of poor and dependent people lacking in
basic needs such as adequate health care and an acceptable
quality of life.

We are a state with an abundance of all of the basic natural resources—productive land, minerals, water, timber,
clean air, a benign climate—that should make it one of the
nation's richest areas. The depressing fact is that it has the
nation's lowest per capita income. It is the place that has
produced some of the world's great writers, musicians, and
literary figures. Yet at the same time we have one of the highest percentages of functionally illiterate adults. That led the
late Chancellor Porter Fortune of Ole Miss to facetiously re-
mark that Mississippians may not be able to read but they

surely can write. Mississippi is arguably the state that has most fiercely resisted change, but it is also the place that has been most fundamentally affected by change, particularly in terms of race relations.

However, the greatest paradox of all may be that despite the obvious benefits that have come from federal programs which have played such an indispensable part in improving the quality of life for so many of our citizens, we have come to regard the federal government with increased disdain. Historically, much of that disdain was related to the issue of racial segregation, which for so long held us, black and white alike, in bondage.

Now, though, after finally ridding ourselves of the burden of Jim Crow, there still remains a reluctance to confront the reality that we still have so much ground to make up in achieving economic and social parity for our state. The lofty goals that we have set in recent years cannot be achieved against a backdrop of continuing neglect of our human resources and a pattern of distressingly unequal economic development, where the gap between the affluent and the poor is widening.

The unhappy truth is that as long as we have and continue to have so many undereducated and, therefore, so many underproductive people, Mississippi is going to be poorer than the rest of the country. Poorly educated people translate into poor people. Adequate education is the one thing that will break the cycle of poverty that has haunted us for so long.

The solution to these problems, however, as Professor Weber points out in this volume, cannot be found in simplistic and superficial actions. Otherwise we would have solved them already. He argues that the change that actually matters must be fundamentally deeper and broader than what we have tried before. He believes as I do that there must be a basic change in how we go about setting our priorities and embracing the social contract that we profess to live under.

It will serve us to step back now and look at Mississippi, as this book does, from the perspective of examining the basis of our past mistakes and our experiences in the mindset of resistance to change. More of our leaders in politics, business, and civic affairs must be willing to do that. That will take courage and vision that too often has been lacking before. We must see to it that more citizens, and especially our young citizens, have a clear understanding of how we got to where we are. There is not enough of this kind of teaching and learning going on. Too many of our most able and promising young men and women have only a passing acquaintance with the events and heroes that have shaped our history. So few really know much about how our government came together in the first place. They do not appreciate how compromise played such a vital role in the framing of the US Constitution.

The lack of civic learning and an understanding of our historical background can be a fatal flaw in the capacity of these future leaders to lead. Without a knowledge of what has gone before, they may well fall into the trap of repeating the old mistakes and ignoring the lessons that earlier generations paid so dearly to learn.

We must all clearly understand that public and civic leadership is never an easy road to travel. There are many stresses and strains these days. It is easy for us to get split up over issues about which many people feel deeply. There are full-time practitioners in politics and in the media and even in some church groups who fan the flames of division and discord.

We must not let ourselves succumb to the tendency to demonize those who see things through different eyes, based usually on different life experiences. Sometime we have to walk in someone else's shoes for a while to understand where that person is coming from.

My perspective is that the best way to overcome these stresses is through sharing experiences—working with others and recognizing that we are all in this together and that what we have in common is so much greater than the things that divide us. As we work with other people who may be different from us, the old barriers and old stereotypes begin to fade away.

All of us must be willing to speak out against bigotry and intolerance and injustice. We must seek to find worth in every person. That is how we pay our dues for the privilege of living in a free society. That is how we can pass on to the next generation a better state than the one we inherited.

Of all the qualities that I believe are necessary for building a more just and productive state, the most important are optimism and persistence. They must be accompanied, of course, by competence and compassion. The application of those qualities can overcome the cynicism and apathy that have been the downfall of so many societies.

That is a lesson for all of us. We can let the naysayers and cynics destroy our vision and close our minds to the choices we have, or we can work to make our state and country more livable for everyone. This should be a challenge that more of us welcome. To feel that one is a participant in building up one's community, especially in times of challenge and hardship, can be the key to a fulfilling life. Instead of fantasizing about glories that never were or might have been, let us concentrate and transmit our energies to the here and now and to the what can be.

At a time when so many narrowly focused special interest groups abound, more of us should consider ourselves as lobbyists for the public interest. We need to be involved in creating constituencies for quality education, for adequate health care, for the preservation of a livable environment, and for the formation of more responsive structures of government.

We must bring together diverse constituencies and serve as a bridge between people and groups representing different interests but who have more in common than they may know. We must help communities identify their local strengths and resources. That is primarily a matter of stimulating vision where none has existed by creating, educating, informing, and building community leadership.

Helping to establish models of programs that work, sharing successes, transmitting a spark of know-how—these must be our tasks. All of this calls for a continuing process of self-education and civic education. This must be true education not in sound bites and slogans but in a serious understanding of our responsibilities in the preservation and perpetuation of our free society.

We need all the help we can get to protect us from the raw and uncompromising pressures of biased or uninformed public opinion that rob us of our individuality and close our minds. We must do more to make reasonable voices heard. We must support and encourage honest, conscientious public officials to take principled stands even when those stands may pinch our own toes. None of us ought to expect politicians to deliver everything we want.

In the increasingly complex and diverse society in which we now find ourselves living, very few public issues have clear-cut answers. It is the test of responsible citizenship to find a way to accommodate differences in a reasonable way. Honorable compromise has always been a necessary element in good leadership. Some naïve people regard it as a sign of weakness. Actually, it may involve great courage. It involves recognizing that most issues have two or more sides. Otherwise, nothing gets done. That kind of political gridlock is happening too often these days. We must remember that none of us has a totally omniscient and clairvoyant view of the issues that confront us. For most of us, our perceptions and opinions have emanated from our life experiences and the influences of our family, teachers, writers, and public leaders. We must, therefore, understand how important it is to use that acquired knowledge plus our own common sense to weigh and explore and be open to new and better ideas and ways of doing things. We must not be afraid to examine the bases of our beliefs.

Rather than being fearful and pessimistic about our future here in Mississippi and in America, I regard this as being the time when we come together and put behind us once and for all the divisive and negative elements that have delayed the fulfillment of our hopes and dreams. This volume contains the blueprint to move us to the achievement of those worthy goals.

Jackson, MS, August 27, 2014

UNITING MISSISSIPPI

INTRODUCTION

In the richest country in the world, some states are still home to deep poverty. The Children's Defense Fund notes that Mississippi has the worst child poverty rate in the country, at 31.8 percent.[1] The Annie E. Casey Foundation's Kids Count index ranked Mississippi in last place among the states with regard to child well-being, based on metrics including health, teenage pregnancy, drug and alcohol abuse, poverty, and death rates.[2]

To be sure, landing in last place on an elite list may not always be an indictment. People who arrive in last place at the Olympics are still remarkable runners. However, a few of the Kids Count index results demonstrate the problems for Mississippi's position in various rankings. In 2011, Mississippi had a 10.7 percent unemployment rate, with many areas of the state falling between a 15.2 and a 19 percent rate. Nearly 43.8 percent of children in the state live in single-parent families. The overall high school graduation rate is 73.7 percent,[3] but this metric is deceptive and depends on who is counted in the measure. For example, in a 2007 report, one county saw only 32 percent of high school freshmen make it to their senior year.[4] Finally, while the state's overall infant mortality rate is 9.8 per thousand each year, in poor counties like Tunica and Montgomery, the rates are 22.9 and 29.2 per thousand, respectively. Compare these numbers with another rural state, Iowa, in which the unemployment rate is 5.9 percent and the infant mortality rate is 4.7 each year per thousand, rising no higher than 13.3 in a single county.[5]

In short, in the pockets of deep poverty, Mississippians' lives are profoundly more difficult than in the wealthier areas and exhibit traits one would not expect to see in the wealthiest country in the world.

In education, the state fares similarly. According to Mississippi reporter Sid Salter in the *Desoto Times Tribune*, "As of 2011 accountability results, 67 of Mississippi's 152 school districts, or just over 44 percent, were rated either academic watch, low performing, at risk of failing, or failing."[6]

Even nations of great wealth and democratic governance face profound challenges, particularly when it comes to simply providing an adequate educational foundation for all citizens. Concern about these issues is not guided by a desire for complete equality of conditions, but for equal access to a quality education. Scholars such as John Rawls have argued that differences in wealth are consistent with a just society, so long as the advantage of the few does not come at the diminishment of the quality of life or of life opportunities for the least advantaged citizens.[7]

Equality is an important democratic ideal, but it is often oversimplified. John Dewey, one of America's most influential democratic philosophers, argued that we are all equal because we are individuals, because we are all different. Equality does not mean our lives or conditions should be the same. Instead, we should think of equality in relation to our opportunities to develop and flourish as individuals. In this way, Dewey's philosophy was sympathetic with the spirit of Rawls's point about differences in wealth. Dewey believed that the great wealth of the United States meant that no children should have to grow up in environments blighted by poverty, that such conditions are most unnecessary here.[8]

As a college professor in Mississippi, I have found the

problems in education here to be palpable and intertwined with poverty.[9] My experience has surprised me, given that the United States has generated some of the most important and innovative philosophical ideas about education, particularly in Dewey's philosophy. These facts together led me to research the confluence of Mississippi's problems in poverty, education, and democracy. These are problem areas for the state, but more importantly they are opportunities for leadership. States that are wealthy, healthy, and united need management to keep their ships sailing on the course already set. No state is without its problems, but Mississippi offers the far greater opportunity. Leadership here can yield great progress. I hope that this book inspires optimism for progress, not just another grim account of the state's deficits. At the same time, optimism for the future will be superficial and ineffectual without an honest and careful look at the problems we face.

While studying poverty, education, and democracy in Mississippi, I simultaneously worked on developing a theory of democratic leadership. As a pragmatic philosopher, I believe that my theories would be meaningless if they could not be applied to the real world. When I finished work on my theory of democratic leadership, therefore, I felt that the logical next step would be to apply my theory to my home state of Mississippi. This book resulted from wondering what lessons, if any, could be drawn from the values of democratic leadership for the sake of pursuing a prosperous and bright future for Mississippi. And since I wanted to test my theory of democratic leadership, it made sense to begin where democracy faces some of its great difficulties. As the opening epigraph from William Faulkner declares, "To understand the world, you have to understand a place like Mississippi."[10] If we adapt Faulkner's maxim, we might suggest that to understand democratic leadership, we must consider what it can contribute in a place as complex as Mississippi.

In developing my theory of democratic leadership, I returned to one of the most influential moral and political philosophers who ever lived, Plato. Plato's *Republic* contains invaluable lessons for living and leading well, even if he was also wrongheaded about many things. It was my aim to learn from what Plato was right about, namely his division of the cardinal virtues of leadership—*wisdom, courage, moderation,* and *justice*—while updating those elements of Plato's insights that conflict with democracy. To the latter end, I turned to the great democratic philosopher, John Dewey, as well as more recent philosophers inspired by his work. Through a study of Plato and Dewey, I proposed a general definition of good leadership that calls it *the application of wisdom and justice with courage and moderation to the guidance of human conduct.* Long definitions are cumbersome, so I abbreviated it: Good leadership is: *judicious yet courageous guidance.* With Dewey's help, I reconstructed Plato's understanding of these virtues to adapt them for the democratic era. My explanation of this further step will wait until chapter 3. My aim is to apply this new theory of leadership, one which is especially infused with democratic values, to the challenges and potential for Mississippi's progress. I argue that each of the lessons on the virtues drawn from Plato's *Republic* and adapted for the democratic context has beneficial implications for the judicious yet courageous guidance of Mississippi's future.

I will begin in chapter 1 as I did when I first arrived in Mississippi, looking to theories of economic growth in the hopes that they might alleviate the state's poverty-related problems. I argue in that chapter that focusing on the economy puts the cart before the horse in terms of addressing Mississippi's challenges. While economist Benjamin Friedman contends in *The Moral Consequences of Economic Growth* (2005) that we should think about moral development as a consequence of economic growth,[11] I have come to think the reverse is necessary for Mississippi—that economic growth should be considered the product of moral growth. Friedman's arguments encounter difficulty in communities with complex histories, such as in Mississippi or in South Africa.[12] In states like Mississippi, changes in moral conditions must be pursued in order for the economy to grow and flourish. The cause for optimism here is that Mississippi's stock has been undervalued. Investments of leadership that succeed in moving people out of poverty would reap far greater rewards than opportunities for change in other states.

After presenting my challenges to Friedman's understanding of moral growth in chapter 1, I offer a picture of educational conditions in the state in chapter 2. Education is commonly considered one of the avenues for development but is in the first place a matter of moral growth that opens opportunities for economic growth. Through education we develop as persons. Former Mississippi governor William Winter has often said that "the only road out of poverty runs by the schoolhouse door."[13] Nevertheless, there is an apparent catch-22 in Mississippi, in which the substantial hurdles of poverty frustrate educational progress, in turn impeding the economic growth necessary for improving educational attainment. I argue in chapter 2 that these problems can be surmounted, but that they must first be identified correctly.

In chapter 3, I return to my theory of democratic leadership to introduce the ways in which each of the key virtues of good democratic leadership can contribute to addressing entrenched social problems. I present in a nutshell and in plain English how I came to develop my theory of democratic leadership in prior work.

Next, in chapters 4, 5, 6, and 7, I attend to the key virtues of democratic leadership, focusing in each case on practical areas of application in which progress can be pursued. Chapter 4 concerns the value of wisdom in leadership, in the democratic form of open and engaged public inquiry, drawing on the greatest evidence available. Chapter 5 covers the virtue of courage, understood especially in terms of the will to experiment, to try new ways and efforts. Chapter 6 focuses on unity, interpreted as aiming for and building on the common good despite differences and historical division. Chapter 7 rounds off my discussion of the virtues with attention to justice, democratically regarded as respect for the dignity and worth of each person. Chapter 8 steps back from these key lessons to consider briefly some particular directions for policy initiatives that will foster the democratic virtues. The measures I propose are not simple, short-term, or easy. I appreciate that it will take time for the will to grow in order to make these steps a reality. If Mississippians want progress, however, we must sincerely engage in a public conversation about the state's future. This book aims to offer only a step in that process.

In the Appendixes, I have included a number of the op-ed essays I have written in an effort to spark discussion and to advocate for causes that I champion in this book. These pieces are offered as examples of small steps that individuals can contribute. I believe that they add some credibility, furthermore, to the idea that the concepts developed in this book have found some small degree of purchase in public discourse. As Dewey once wrote to a friend and colleague, journalism is a fascinating demonstration of the cash value of ideas.[14] Dewey was among America's greatest public philosophers. Following his example led me to write for newspapers from time to time. The Appendixes accordingly consist of seven gathered articles from newspapers and periodicals. Newspapers and various outlets for public discourse are the spheres in which Mississippians can reconstruct the culture underlying the lingering symptoms of the state's troubled history. They are also the place for thinking optimistically and positively about what the state might become, building on strengths and potential for progress. These tasks together represent an ideal context for applying and testing my theory of democratic leadership, which I hope has valuable contributions to offer for Mississippi's future.

1.

RETHINKING
ECONOMIC GROWTH

Who doesn't want economic growth? A quick look at state government websites for rural and poor regions suggests that economic growth is a fundamental goal of local administrations.[1] We have chambers of commerce, economic councils, small business development centers, business incubators, and much more. Local and state governments spend an enormous amount of their time on issues of economic development. This may be true to a greater extent in states like Mississippi, Alabama, and Wyoming than in wealthier places like New York or California, though I suspect leaders in the latter states would disagree. Some cities and states have far larger populations and hence a much greater tax base or more robust economy already for addressing the many social needs that democracy demands. Other states are explicit about the central role of economic growth in local governments' pursuits. Mississippi, for example, is one of the poorest states. While the national poverty rate in 2011 was 15 percent, in Mississippi the rate was 22.6 percent—the highest in the country, according to CNN.[2] It should come as no surprise, therefore, that when we look to Mississippi's state activities, countless efforts aim to build the economy.

Capitalist values are frequently criticized among academics. We all know that there are activities through which business can cause great harm. Some have criticized Walmart for devastating small, locally owned businesses.[3] There is a perception, however correct or inaccurate, that it is the rare scholar who defends business and the pursuit of economic growth. In my experience, I have known many such scholars. Nevertheless, in 1998, libertarian and Harvard philosopher Robert Nozick authored an essay asking, "Why Do Intellectuals Oppose Capitalism?"[4] One need not be a libertarian or a conservative to believe in the value of economic growth. Economist Benjamin Friedman makes a clear case that economic growth is a value for liberal and conservative moral theorists alike. While I also can appreciate the value of economic growth for enabling citizens to rise out of poverty and to pursue their life plans and happiness, I believe that Friedman's thesis runs the wrong direction when applied to Mississippi.

In *The Moral Consequences of Economic Growth*, Friedman argues that economic growth is desirable not simply for its material consequences, but for its moral consequences as well. In several cases, especially the ones that Friedman carefully chooses as evidence—including Britain, France, Germany, and the United States during and after the Great Depression—I believe that Friedman presents a compelling argument. There are, however, several problems with how he does so. Friedman claims that it is not just any kind of economic growth that promotes moral growth. He qualifies carefully what he means by economic growth, calling it "a rising standard of living for the clear majority of citizens."[5] He then goes on to say that when this growth occurs, it occasions the advancement of what he calls "moral growth." He defines this progress as expanding "openness of opportunity, tolerance, economic and social mobility, fairness, and democracy."[6] While these things all sound quite good, and the moral and democratic values that Friedman extols are values that I share, he seems to be finding fur where there is a bear—discovering something implicit in the things he selected to examine. Friedman stacks the deck in favor of lauding economic growth by defining it as a more desirable, democratic kind in the first place. He excludes undesirable patterns of economic change easily labeled "growth," because they are not part of a value-added or free market. Take, for instance, Saudi Arabia's economy, which surely has boomed immensely in the last hundred years. The standard of living may not have risen in such places for a clear majority of citizens, however, and there has been stagnation in some conditions, such as in the unequal treatment of women.[7] Friedman explains that he can set aside such problematic cases for his view because they are due to resource-extraction.

Some places cause trouble for Friedman's hypothesis when considered as examples. In an article titled "A Contribution to the Empirics of Economic Growth" (1992), authors N. Gregory Mankiw, David Romer, and David N. Weil explain that when testing growth models, they "exclude the oil producers because the bulk of recorded GDP for these countries represents the extraction of existing resources, not value added; one should not expect standard growth models to account for measured GDP in these countries."[8] While different kinds of growth will have varied effects, it seems to me—and more importantly to a great many economists[9]—that it is not strange to call the last fifty to one hundred years of Saudi Arabian history a time of vast economic growth. In addition, it is undeniable that there have been fast changes to some people's way of life, at least in terms of material conditions, in Saudi Arabia, whether or not cultural or social conditions have changed much.[10] While certain scholars may want to restrict their definitions of economic growth, the important implication is that ultimately what is valuable is a *certain kind* of economic growth, namely that which benefits all in a substantial way. The challenge is to discern in advance which efforts to stimulate economic growth will yield *good* growth—the kind that raises the standard of living for all—rather than some other form. In many rural and poor regions, furthermore, if there is interest in bringing business to town, it sounds adversarial to question the nature of the growth that will result, even if it would be a good matter to consider. Such questions are dismissed as if they are against economic growth, against progress. Economic growth is powerful because it enhances people's abilities to pursue their own ends. When such growth is not widespread, not shared, gaps between rich and poor are widened and some goods become even harder for the poor to obtain.[11]

There are also many places in which a number of people have gotten very rich from natural resources, while their fellow citizens remain very poor—not what Friedman would consider good growth. South Africa is one complicated example, given the country's history of British colonization and apartheid.[12] In a number of instances, economic growth of one form or another has been accompanied by gross unfairness, authoritarianism, limited opportunity, and oppression. Thus, since Friedman picked as his measure of economic growth a democratic and fair distribution of improved standards of living, it should be of no surprise that these conditions accompany fair social practices, and that his model excludes countries like Saudi Arabia and South Africa from consideration. Thus, those societies that select forms of economic growth that benefit all are either good for all by chance, or by design already, given a morally good social structure and government.

It is important for me to qualify here that various kinds of economic growth may be good, or at least not harmful—

consistent with the rise in quality of life for all. Not every business or economic effort needs to address this important democratic mission. Nevertheless, the quality of life of all citizens should be motivating for overarching economic goals and policies.

As I have said, there are many values I share with Friedman. Openness, tolerance, and democratic values all should be norms in societies made up of a vast mixture of people, such as the United States. These values embody what is necessary for thriving in a place that exhibits what John Rawls has called "reasonable pluralism," where great differences abound among intelligent, reasonable people about some of the fundamental issues of life's purpose, ethical rules, and value.[13] At the same time, when a society or a community does not appreciate the "fact of reasonable pluralism," or when it is divided by ethnic or racial prejudice, then it is difficult for the community to break out of its traditions of subjugation. This is not only the case for many women in oppressive states, but also for poor persons in wealthy countries, such as some Mississippians, who lack the educational opportunities requisite for the openness of opportunity, tolerance, and other democratic values that Friedman trumpets. In fact, in 2012 CNN reported that US "Federal civil rights lawyers filed suit . . . against Meridian, Mississippi, and other defendants for operating what the government calls a school-to-prison pipeline in which students are denied basic constitutional rights, sent to court and incarcerated for minor school offenses."[14] In its suit against Meridian, the federal government alleged that citizens lacked just the kind of openness of opportunity and fairness that Friedman calls for—and this in the wealthy United States of America. The case in Meridian is an example of a failure to embody the values that Friedman esteems as sought-after consequences of economic growth—according to his view. It is unclear, however, that such unfair and troubling school practices would end for the poor and minority students in Meridian just because of increase economic growth on its own. Instead, better school practices could well yield greater graduation rates, lesser incarceration, and consequently stronger economic outcomes, I argue.

There are cases that do not fit Friedman's theory so nicely, like Meridian, Mississippi. Certain poor regions, such as Mississippi, have been engaged in countless efforts to foster economic growth, some of which have borne fruit, such as in the pursuit of automobile manufacturing.[15] Still, such growth has been slow and is consistent with retaining the state's many pockets of deep poverty and inequality. If Friedman's thinking is wrong, or at least unhelpful, for leading us to prioritize the pursuit of economic growth for the sake of moral progress, however, then we must instead first look to growing the moral capacities, opportunities, and quality of life of people living in the poorest regions of places like Mississippi. Only then can we truly achieve success in stimulating their economies virtuously. It is in this sense, then, I argue that in some cases we must evaluate our prospects for the economic consequences of moral growth, a reversal of Friedman's message.

These ideas do not only speak in the abstract. The consequence of accepting the reversal that I propose calls for a rethinking of some traditional and largely unsuccessful approaches to economic growth. For example, there is a much repeated and oversimplified belief that lower taxes yield economic growth. Alan Reynolds, senior fellow with the Cato Institute, has summarized the maxim in his article, "Lower Tax Rates Mean Faster Economic Growth."[16] Critics of this outlook, like Cornel West, have labeled such views "free-market fundamentalism."[17] Reynolds's claim is worth considering, since it is so common a view. It is also quite simple and clear. The places that have lower taxes should grow economically at a faster rate than other regions, according to Reynolds's theory. If Reynolds's claim were correct, however, one would expect to see states with the lowest taxes growing quickly and thriving.[18] If a state has long been among those with the lowest tax burdens, furthermore, one could reasonably expect it to be among the richer states in the nation or at least not among the poorest states. Unfortunately for Reynolds's claim, the converse is the case. Mississippi has long been a state with some of the lowest taxes in the nation and was called in a 2012 Bloomberg report the state with the lowest tax burden.[19] Nevertheless, it is one of the poorest states in the country. One might think that perhaps Mississippi is an exception, but similar conditions are true also for South Carolina, Alabama, Tennessee, and Alaska.[20]

It is straightforward logic to suggest that if all else were equal, people would tend to pick those benefits which come with the lowest costs, such as states with lower taxes. Especially in states like Mississippi and Alabama, however, the idea that "all else is equal" is surely false. The South— and in particular Louisiana, Mississippi, Alabama, Georgia, and South Carolina—are famous for "underinvestment in infrastructure and education."[21] Alabama and Mississippi have particularly low taxes and consequently low per pupil spending on public education. It should be no surprise that their educational outcomes are correspondingly worse. When businesses consider relocating and look at states like Mississippi and Alabama, those companies that are concerned about having an educated workforce and strong infrastructure for various needs and services will look to other states, even if the corresponding tax burden is higher elsewhere. This is not true of all industries, as I have suggested in relation to some exceptions, like car manufacturers, but the company relocations to date have not driven down the poverty rate.[22] I believe that this is partly due to the state's unwillingness to invest seriously in infrastructure, and especially on educational preparation of the whole workforce.

The proper way to appreciate the need for public investment in education and other infrastructural services and needs, along with the general desirability of lower taxes, is to think of the sort of nexus that applies in studies of supply and demand curves, where maximization of economic benefit comes from matching the right supply for the demand in just the right way. Similarly, Mississippi has long competed as the cheapest place to live with respect to taxes. That approach alone has been largely unsuccessful,[23] and the state remains deeply poor, comparatively. Therefore, a better balance must be sought, and the fear that greater public expenditures and thus tax rates will reduce the incentive for businesses to relocate to Mississippi may in fact be proven false, at least to a point. In this sense, we can see that the excessive prioritization of minimalist taxation in the name of economic development may in fact be a causal force undermining the state's ability to support its public endeavors sufficiently. This is why we must rethink Friedman's claim when it comes to places like Mississippi. Mississippi's challenges suggest that moral growth, such as in the form of increasing investment in education to provide not only an adequate but a strong or excellent education for all citizens, will result in maximized benefits in terms of quality of life and opportunities for all and economic conditions attractive to investment and businesses. If my hypothesis proves correct, then, the test will show that in fact desirable economic growth *is a consequence* of moral growth.

2.

EDUCATION IN MISSISSIPPI

Childhood blighted through poverty and hardship is an unpardonable sin in this the only nation in the world whose national income is sufficient to afford a decent standard of living to all within its borders. Protection of childhood is implicit in the expression "Peace on earth, good will to man."

—John Dewey, "Attacks Wage Disparity," December 26, 1929[1]

I moved to Mississippi after completing a dissertation featuring in part the work of John Dewey, the scholar dubbed America's philosopher and famed for contributions in areas including ethics, politics, and especially education.[2] According to Robert Westbrook's authoritative study, Dewey "would become the most important philosopher in American history."[3] Among Dewey's most influential contributions were his writings on education. Although Westbrook called Dewey's impact on public education limited,[4] Dewey's *Democracy and Education* (1916) became a symbol and guide for the champions of public education. Dewey's influence earned him the title "the Patron Saint of Schools."[5] The *New York Times* even called him "foremost among educators in the country."[6] It is fair to say that Dewey was a vocal and important figure advancing an American philosophy of education, one which inspired many around the world,[7] and for which he was widely lauded. Dewey was even depicted in a stained-glass window, by the Loire Studios of Chartres, created for the Grace Cathedral in San Francisco—reflecting the "Patron Saint of Schools" label.[8]

Before the slow process of the democratization of education in America, education was largely private, for the few
with means to obtain it, and authoritarian in style. Students
were taught primarily the skills of memorization and rep-
etition and were discouraged from both criticism of traditional authorities and creativity not bound within strict limits. Against these traditions and practices, Dewey and other
advocates for democratizing education argued for a liberal
educational system and approach, one open to all—*public*
education—and fundamental to democracy.

Dewey's educational philosophy built on Thomas Jefferson's understanding of the vital role of education.[9] Jefferson wrote to Madison that we must "educate and inform
the whole mass of the people, enable them to see that it is
in their interest to preserve peace and order, and they will
preserve it. . . . They are the only sure reliance for the preservation of our liberty. . . . [Informed citizens] are the most
legitimate engine of government."[10] Jefferson's instruction
motivates one of my central views about democratic leadership. Given Jefferson's inspiration and the needs of democracy, the people must contribute to leadership, not defer-
ring or abnegating their responsibilities for leadership just
because we elect particular individuals for public office.
While Jefferson was an inspiration in word while not everywhere in deed—such as in his tolerance of and participation in the institution of slavery[11]—Dewey championed this
Jeffersonian insight about education. Dewey explained that
we must reject Plato's undemocratic caste system in favor of
democratic values, applying them especially to education.

In Mississippi today, the differences between the public schools of the rich and of the poor, between the white
and the black schools, smack of the caste system that democracy is supposed to leave behind. The problem is so

profound here that even in late 2012, an extended article in *The Atlantic* called attention to the state's segregated academies, which the author says are still going strong.[12] There is much more to be done to render Mississippi truly democratic, therefore, especially in the area of education.

Education is vital for the task of uniting Mississippi through democratic leadership for two reasons. First, leadership must attend to these problems in education, through which undemocratic practices are causes of injustice. Second, attending to education is a step in the process of fostering the next generation of leaders. Dewey explained this latter ideal, writing that "the society of which the child is to be a member is, in the United States, a democratic and progressive society. The child must be educated for leadership as well as for obedience. He [or she] must have power of self-direction and power of directing others, powers of administration, ability to assume positions of responsibility. This necessity of educating for leadership is as great on the industrial side as on the political side."[13] Educating all citizens for leadership would mean a rejection of the caste system and undemocratic values. It would mean moral growth in the sense that I had in mind in chapter 1.

One of the ways education can be undemocratic is in treating certain classes of people as basic laborers only, as unfit for a liberal arts education. Dewey believed that there was nothing wrong with vocational training itself, such as what we often find as a focus in community colleges. He would object, however, to denying people a fuller, liberal education for democratic citizenship, or training people for vocations without a broader education. The idea is that a free society is something that must be cultivated. A liberal education is vital for the maintenance of freedom and the pursuit of justice. In this context, it is important to remember that "liberal education" refers to an education in the arts necessary for nurturing and maintaining a free people, a free society. Free people uneducated in what it takes to preserve freedom can very quickly lose their liberty. Not only is liberal arts education crucial for democracy, therefore, but the education for which Dewey advocated must be infused with the values of democracy, with the arts that foster individuality, personal growth, and freedom.

In light of Dewey's philosophy of democracy and education, Mississippi's problems appear all the more troubling. There have been extensive criticisms of American public education since its inception.[14] Of late, more and more schools have caused alarm for their poor graduation rates, low test scores, and increasing violence. In pockets of America, including Mississippi, many public high schools graduate only 60 to 75 percent of students, and in some troubled areas the results are considerably lower.[15] Graduation rates are ambiguous, though, since they sometimes refer to students who are seniors and graduate, while other reports refer to freshmen who eventually graduate. The former number will always be far larger than the latter, given attrition between grades nine and eleven. At one time, the Canton County School District yielded only a 32 percent retention of its freshmen all the way to their senior year.[16] Its numbers have improved, fortunately,[17] but later in the 2010–2011 school year, the Amite County High School and the West Oktibbeha County High School—to name just a few examples—had graduation rates of 44 percent and 47.5 percent, respectively.[18] In short, there are many struggling schools that could serve as examples here.

While these problems are certainly serious, one critic of Dewey's theories of democratic education is quick to blame the philosopher for problems that are more likely rooted in causes like poverty, prejudice, and systemic racism.[19] A clear illustration that the roots of these problems feed from racism and poverty, and not Dewey's philosophy, comes from a 2010 *Time* article by Nate Jones, titled "Want to Be Class President in Mississippi? You Need to Be White." The author highlights a number of ways in which the state is still "living in the past."[20] Jones continues, "Segregation is still alive and well in parts of America. At Nettleton Middle School in Nettleton, Mississippi, students are forbidden from running for certain student government positions if their skin is the wrong color. Each year, three of the four executive positions are set aside for white students; one of the four is set aside for a black student."[21] In an update to the piece later that year, Jones writes, "The district has posted a new statement saying the policy will be discontinued."[22] Aside from stories like these, consider that it has been headline news around the country in recent years when some Mississippi schools have held their first interracial proms.[23] The consequences in educational results of the overall culture of low expectations and racism in the state are profound. They include the fact that even those who do graduate from high school often find themselves unprepared for college.[24]

The counties in Mississippi in which school districts are failing and in which citizens live in areas of concentrated poverty largely overlap, and the areas are simultaneously divided along racial lines as well. For evidence, consider the Associated Press's analysis of "Dropout Factories" from 2007.[25] The three Mississippi school districts with the lowest retention rates of freshmen who reach their senior year, from 32 to 45 percent, also have student bodies that are 95.74 to 99.77 percent African American.[26] The racial divide that aligns with enormous differences in educational attainment in the state recalls the troubling caste system at work in Plato's day, and most aggressively intensified in America's long history of chattel slavery. The federal government's suit against Meridian, Mississippi, which I discussed in chapter 1, confirms my worry.[27]

Complicating matters with regard to assessing and improving schools, some states inflate their books to make themselves look better with regard to key metrics, such as graduation rates. This only makes it more difficult to assess the scope of a state's problems. Reporting for the *New York Times* in a 2008 article, "States' Inflated Data Obscure Epidemic of School Dropouts," Sam Dillon explained his finding at the time that "Mississippi keeps two sets of books."[28] In addition, Peter Whoriskey's *Washington Post* article, "By the Mississippi Delta, a Whole School Left Behind" (2007), labeled Como, Mississippi's elementary school the most troubled school in America.[29] The school's principal at the time, Versa Brown, recognized that "we're just light-years behind." Whoriskey goes on to cite then–state superintendent of schools, Hank Bounds, writing,

> "Has No Child Left Behind done some good things?
> Sure. . . . But in many places like the Mississippi Delta,
> I would have to say no." He rejected the notion that
> raising test standards—without somehow persuading
> legions of motivated teachers to move in—would help
> students. "It's easy to put your bow tie on every day
> and say 'if Mississippi would just do X then you would
> see Y results,'" he said.[30]

It is important to appreciate Bounds's point. For a long time, people have offered focused suggestions about adjusting this or that particular feature of a school or its system. It is surely true that many things have been tried, though not all, and it is also true that it is a great challenge to attract high quality teachers to places like Como, Mississippi—population 1,279, as of the 2010 US Census.[31] What Bounds seems to be pointing out is that what is required for real change must be a serious effort, culturally and financially speaking, to attract quality teachers to remote and poor areas of the state.

In the last few years, Mississippi's standing has improved, but only so far. The *Atlanta Journal-Constitution*'s Maureen Downey asked in 2012, "Remember when Georgia used to say 'Thank God for Mississippi and Alabama?'"[32] It turns out that Georgia's schools have begun to produce even more troubling results than Mississippi's on some metrics. At the same time, no longer resting at the bottom is not the same as an improvement. Such changes can make Mississippi look better just because other places decline. While Mississippi's graduation rates have improved somewhat in recent years,[33] a high school degree that leaves one unprepared for higher education suggests a social stratification, a classification of people. This is especially troubling when differences are systematically noticeable for certain groups. Mississippi students ranked in last place in the 2012 state comparisons of the ACT, a standardized test measuring college preparedness, and while white students' average score of 21 out of a possible 36 is not nationally competitive, black students' average score of 16 illustrates my cause for concern.[34]

In the face of educational difficulties, some blame government, administrators, Dewey, or the lack of prayer in school for the state's problems.[35] A vast commonality is observable, however, in poorly performing schools. Their students generally live in deep poverty.[36] Populations living in poverty encounter challenges that raise costs for providing a quality education, and in contexts in which it is harder to garner the will of the wider public to increase support. A report by Doris Nhan in the *National Journal* is headlined "How Much States Spend on Their Kids Really Does Matter." Nhan notes that "states that spent the least per student in 2009 were ranked fairly low on education."[37] Mississippi spent $9,700 per pupil for the year, near the low end of the spectrum in the country, and scored in the lowest category in educational outcomes.[38] According to 2009 data, Wyoming spent the most per pupil, at $18,068, though it still only ranked twenty-ninth in quality, and the national average that year was $11,665.[39] Wyoming reveals that money cannot guarantee top performance. We must remember, however, that where challenges are great, costs are higher. Wyoming certainly has shown its commitment to education despite the challenges for it in highly rural states. As with many problems, the deeper the challenge, the more expensive problems can be to fix.

In my early work on the topic of Mississippi's educational challenges, it seemed clear to me that for a number of poor areas, if we hope to improve educational practices and performance, we must see our goal as including the pursuit of economic growth for the poor. Thus, for some time, my research focused on how to achieve economic growth in conditions of educational frustration. Great problems arise, however, for the pursuit of economic growth in areas with poor educational systems. So leaders of public policy face an apparent catch-22—a view I presented in the essay reprinted here as Appendix 2. I have argued that the catch-22 can be overcome by looking to the common roots of both parts of the dilemma in a culture that accepts failure.[40] But doing so requires appreciating the depth of the difficulty involved.

Eric F. Dubow and Maria F. Ippolito reveal, as the title of their 1994 article indicates, the "Effects of Poverty and Quality of the Home Environment on Changes in the Academic and Behavioral Adjustment of Elementary School-Age Children."[41] According to Dubow and Ippolito, "Prior poverty status . . . predicted decreases in math and reading scores and increases in antisocial behavior. . . . The relation between parental [socioeconomic status (SES)] and children's academic achievement is well documented . . . , [with] 200 studies of SES as a correlate of individual academic achievement."[42] The effort to improve education in Mississippi, therefore, appears correlative to growing the economy. If it were in fact the case that students living in poverty cannot succeed in any significant numbers, given their high likelihood of educational frustration, then the catch-22 would be insurmountable. There is hope, however, evident in some remarkable experimental charter schools that have shown what students from poor backgrounds can do in the right circumstances. I add here that even if charter schools themselves are not the answer, successful examples of them point to the potential for change. I must also emphasize here that recognizing some successes in charter schools does not imply that charter policies are the solution for education in Mississippi. The evidence of successful young people who succeed educationally despite living in poverty is the important point I mean to emphasize. What matters and is of value in such examples concerns the potential inherent in investing in and carefully creating the conditions necessary for disadvantaged young people to succeed.

In particular, the Knowledge Is Power Program charter schools (KIPP) in Arkansas's Helena-West Helena school district have proven remarkably successful, and with a student body made up of children who live in poverty and who are nearly all African American. In addition, the KIPP Delta schools, while in Arkansas, are nevertheless in the Mississippi Delta region and are thus quite comparable in nature to the demographics of schools on the Mississippi side of the river.[43] A quick look at benchmark exams demonstrates not only that these KIPP Delta schools have been more successful than their counterparts in the Helena-West Helena school district—the traditional, non-KIPP schools—but also that by eighth grade their students perform well above Arkansas's overall average scores. For two good illustrations, consider first their eleventh grade literacy results from 2012. Statewide, 68 percent of all Arkansas students were proficient, compared with the Helena-West Helena traditional School District's (HWHSD) 34 percent. The KIPP Delta schools' students were 93 percent proficient. Next, and almost as striking, in "multiple grades geometry" performance, the percentage of students scoring proficient or above for eighth graders in the state was 75, the HWHSD's was 39 percent, and the KIPP Delta school's average was 90 percent.[44]

	KIPP Delta Collegiate High School	Helena/West Helena School District	Arkansas
11th Grade Literacy	93%	34%	68%
Multiple Grades Geometry	90%	39%	75%
Multiple Grades Biology	35%	10%	43%

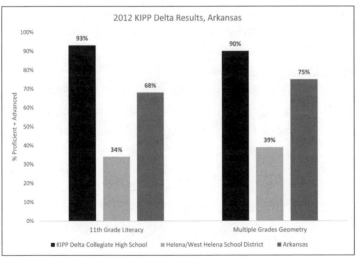

Many people have become advocates for charter schools in Mississippi. The state legislature recently passed legislation to allow them. The reasonable questions are, "What is it that these schools are doing to be successful? Why not implement such insights all over the state?" Successful charter schools attract strong teachers and generally hold longer school days than traditional schools, among other differences. To be sure, they also tend to draw the stronger students out of the traditional public schools, as well as students whose parents are more involved in their education. The point is not that charter schools are the answer, though looking at these various differences could either inform public school practices or the development of new charter schools. Whether charter schools are taken as an avenue for progress or as indicators of reforms needed in public schools, the important lesson is that the KIPP Delta schools show that students raised in deep poverty and in remote and rural parts of the country can be highly successful in school under the right conditions. What I would argue for directly is the establishment of such conditions for all students, especially for disadvantaged and at-risk students. It is certainly important to listen to the critics of charter schools who worry about the young people left behind in failing traditional schools, among other concerns.

In the fall of 2009, I had the chance to visit the Helena-West Helena KIPP Delta schools. It was remarkable how the public charter school appeared to be an oasis in the economically distressed town. In Helena-West Helena, there was grass growing from the sidewalks and countless boarded up buildings. In contrast to the general disarray, once I entered the KIPP Delta Collegiate High School, I found students dressed in blazer topped uniforms.[45] Visiting classrooms, I saw hands shoot up in large numbers when teachers asked questions. What struck me, seeing the KIPP schools in Arkansas, was not the technical design of curriculum, reading levels, or strong teachers, though all of those features are strengths. What was most impressive to me was the clear, intentional, and reinforced culture of success and excellence that the school had established and maintained.

When I visited, the school had only been in operation for a few years and was therefore graduating its first and smallest class, consisting of nineteen students. On my visit, I met with students to talk about the University of Mississippi and to get to know them. They asked me questions about college, professors, and classes. Their eagerness and intelligence were easy to see. In addition, on my way to meet the students, I walked along the corridor of their new building. On the wall was a bulletin board featuring the seniors' acceptance letters from colleges. All students but one at the time had received letters of acceptance to college, and the remaining student simply had not yet received word about his applications. Over the years, the ranks of students in the school have grown consistently, and the school's track record has grown with it. In 2013, the *Clarion Ledger* (Jackson, MS) reported that "Every Arkansas KIPP Delta Grad [Was] Accepted Into College."[46]

As we consider stories like those from the KIPP schools in Arkansas, it is important to keep in mind just how deep the challenges are for Mississippi. In May 2012, Eli Hager, a Teach for America (TFA) teacher in the Mississippi Delta contributed a piece for the *Washington Post* in which he argued that education in the state is, as the article's headline read, "Still Separate and Unequal."[47] He explained that

the Delta is half black and half white, yet the public schools here that are "failing" and "at risk of failing" are

95 percent black, according to data compiled by the US Commission on Civil Rights. Its white academies are just that: purposely all-white, prestigious, and successful. The black public schools, meanwhile, graduate students who are functionally illiterate or who read several grade levels behind those at affluent schools nationally.[48]

The depth of the challenge cannot be overstated. We can see the desire to resist caste differentiation both in Hager's frustration and in the outlook underlying the KIPP schools. The founder of the KIPP Delta schools, Scott Shirley, has argued, in an article titled "For Students, 'Zip Code Does Not Define Destiny'" (2012), that we need not accept the kinds of outcomes that Hager describes.[49] Were Dewey alive today, I believe he would say that present conditions reflect a lack of appreciation for the dignity and worth of each person, a central democratic value disregarded.

The insights that we can draw from the KIPP schools include both the potential for replication of their formal models and, more importantly, of their larger cultural considerations. Until Mississippians no longer accept the conditions that are limiting the potential of poor and African American communities in the state, any small measure for progress will likely do little, as former state superintendent of schools Hank Bounds suggested.[50] There is reason to be cautiously hopeful for change, however. Former governor William Winter has been called the "education governor" for championing and passing the 1982 Mississippi Education Reform Act, which suggests that some profound changes can be achieved.[51] While Winter would be among the first to admit that much more needed and still needs to be done, the act passed during his administration brought about improvements in governance and funding. It also established public funding for kindergarten for all Mississippians. Beyond this, former governor Haley Barbour has said that "Education is the No. 1 economic development issue and the No. 1 quality-of-life issue in our state . . . [and] Education is rightly the No. 1 priority of state government."[52] In addition, the present governor, Phil Bryant, is calling the legislature to increase support for Teach for America and the Mississippi Teacher Corps (MTC) by millions of dollars, even if critics have called these programs only small and partial measures for progress.[53] Democratic leadership in Mississippi must consider how to reform at all levels a culture in the state which has long accepted failure in the schools for poor and minority populations. Not only does democracy demand such reform, but the demonstrated potential for progress is a strong cause for optimism.

3.

DEMOCRATIC LEADERSHIP—DEFINITIONS AND TOOLS

To imagine the possibilities for Mississippi's future, it is vital to address particular problems and policies. While so far I have only scratched the surface of two complex and mutually aggravating overarching problems—poverty and educational frustration—the concepts underlying democratic leadership have some insights to offer for tackling the troubles that Mississippi faces. Before looking at specific challenges in Mississippi, I must clarify what I said in the introduction about leadership in general, and also its democratic form.

As I said in the introduction, I take good leadership in general to be *judicious yet courageous guidance*. This is the abbreviation of the four virtues for the ideal society that we learn from Plato's *Republic*, namely *wisdom, courage, moderation*, and *justice*, summarizing three of the virtues with the term judicious. In the longer version, I called desirable leadership *the application of wisdom and justice with courage and moderation to the guidance of human conduct*. Plato often would offer a complex and precise statement or definition of terms and then follow it up with a crystalized, abbreviated phrase.

In other writings,[1] I have developed my theory of democratic leadership, which adapts my general definition of leadership for democratic contexts and purposes. I call good democratic leadership *respectful experimental inquiry for the common good.* A brief explanation of these definitions is necessary, since the purpose of the present book centers on the practical application of this theory of democratic leadership to Mississippi's challenges. I will begin with a look at the general virtues of leadership and then show how they can best be understood in terms of democratic values.

Wisdom in the general sense—not yet especially democratic—is rooted in knowledge, the best evidence available, and good judgment. Where firmly established science is clear, it should inform wise leadership toward virtuous means and ends for policy.

Courage for Plato means fearing the right things and not the wrong things. It is spirited will guided by wisdom. Spirit without the guidance of wisdom can turn soccer fans violent after games,[2] for example. Plato clarified, furthermore, that courage is not the absence of fear, which would be brashness. We should fear crime, failing schools, and waste in government, among other things. We should not fear baseless criticism or the discomfort that can result from speaking out for what is right. Similarly, if change will take trial and error as well as public investment, and if such change is needed, we must not be afraid to stumble in new endeavors, nor to test the waters in new ventures and investments. Cautious wisdom still ought to guide such efforts. By contrast, inaction accepts deep problems out of fear of small harms—precisely the sort of failure of spirit that Plato had in mind when he called for courage.

The virtue of *moderation* refers to the need to keep a group from becoming so divided that the original unity tears itself apart. Within any political party, there are areas of disagreement. What unites a group is its common set of beliefs and values, not some perfect agreement in all things. A presidential candidate often picks a potential vice president who will help capture those whom the main candidate fails to attract. Therefore, the stronger ticket, the stronger unity, is one in which the two candidates of the same party share some core values but differ on many other points.

Recent times have seen harsh denunciations of moderation, accompanying references to President Reagan's dogged conservatism, for example.[3] Other great fans of Reagan see him differently and have called him a "master of the art of compromise."[4] It is undeniable that without remarkable skill at compromise, at achieving unity through a moderation of differences, Reagan could never have won the landslide victory that he did in 1984—525 Electoral College votes to Walter Mondale's 13. Even people who long for separation or independence from their larger nation, such as those in the Scottish National Party, would have had eventually to reckon with the challenge of unifying and moderating differences among the smaller nation they aimed to become.[5] Without moderation, no unity can be held together. Without it there could be no *United* States of America.

Justice, according to Plato, involves achieving the right balance of the first three virtues. Applied to people rather than to balancing virtues, justice means giving each person his or her due, whether in terms of compensation or punishment. For Plato, a caste system was to direct what each person is due, whereas the values of democracy involve precisely the rejection of a systematic classification of persons as more or less valuable simply based on castes. I will say a bit more about the democratic sense of justice in this chapter, but the important point is to consider what it means for each to get what is his or hers, what he or she is due. We see the democratic spirit in contrast with Plato's view, insofar as democracy prizes social mobility open to all. The rejection of caste systems does not mean that all people are or could be the same. If you value democracy, Dewey thought, we should treat people as the distinct, incomparable individuals that we are. Though it may sound paradoxical on the surface, it is *because* we are all different and irreplaceable that we must be understood as equal individuals, according to Dewey.

For Plato, these four virtues are to be embodied by society's guardians, his term for leaders. Guardians are important, but the term today preserves a paternalistic connotation that treats followers as children, and in a way that conflicts with democratic values. We can feel this sense of the term when we think of what a "legal guardian" represents for minors. Citizens can be policed and directed, but are not happy when, as adults, they are treated too much like children. Therefore, learning from Dewey's writings, I conceptualize leadership instead as a form of guidance, rather than guardianship. Desirable democratic leadership guides human conduct, according to this definition, doing so well or poorly given its adherence to or deviation from the virtues of leadership. In addition, the process of guidance can be shared and is not uniquely or narrowly assigned, as legal guardianship is. The democratic shift that I propose is to focus on the process of leadership, rather than on the leader, since in the democratic sense, leadership can be engaged in by many or all individuals and is not to be thought of as a matter only of a special group, contra Plato. Special responsibilities often must be assigned to individuals in order to make sure that things get done, but insights and guidance can be enhanced whether or not it comes from someone in a position of designated authority.

Keeping the idea of guidance in mind, democratic leadership will need to be wise, courageous, moderate, and just, and to be such in a democratic manner, observing democratic means. For democracy, pursued through tyrannical means, ceases to be democratic. Therefore, *democratic wisdom*, first of all, needs to be understood as a virtue to which all can contribute and which is not relegated only to elite experts. Expertise matters, but the specialist in medicine often does not know "where it hurts." So wisdom must be found in shared and free *inquiry*, even when experts are involved.

Plato believed that the need for courage justified censorship and lying on the part of leaders to minimize people's fears and to condition people to fear what leaders want them to fear. It is not a natural inclination to jump on a grenade, for example, and so people need conditioning, as do soldiers, to have the right reactions that will save the group. In a democracy, we can see courage instead in honesty accompanied by the will to *experiment*, such as in the idea that there is a "laboratory of the states" in the United States. It takes courage to experiment in the pursuit of progress. The fears people have of experimentation require no lying or censorship to allay. In fact, more honest and open information dispels fear. We fear what we do not know and we fear manipulation. In that sense, Plato's strategies for shaping courage were problematic and undemocratic, but we need not follow his example in all things. I have argued in the *Clarion Ledger* that courage was needed to experiment with charter schools in districts where schools are failing—in the essay included here as Appendix 6. The wise thing to do is not always known, and so there are strong forces that work to maintain presently stable conditions. Fear of the unknown in experimentation, however, prevents the development of greater wisdom. It is important for people to fear the maintenance of vice more than the small risk of engaging in targeted experiments for the sake of moral progress. In this sense, when democratic inquiry is engaged in courageously, it is *experimental* and honest. To be sure, one can experiment also with reforms within the Department of Education—charter schools are not the only way. The important point is the need to resist the temptation to perpetuate our present failures because experiments do not always or immediately succeed.

Next, moderation was Plato's virtue by which unity is maintained. The trouble is that Plato was authoritarian and believed that it is acceptable to censor people or to kick them out of your city when their ideas conflict with the rulers' views. *Democratic moderation* involves the recognition that there will be great differences between people. The move to achieve moderation in a democracy is inverted, less focused on the extremities of people's beliefs. Instead, moderation in the democratic sense is the effort to find what is *common* despite differences. Shared values keep groups together, yet it is the controversial points of difference that tend to capture the public's attention, such as with regard to news media. There is no real debate about which side of the street we should drive on in public spaces. There are countless matters such as traffic laws about which Americans are in such profound agreement that they fail to see it as an agreement. In 2013, when polarization prompted a shutdown of the federal government, the bipartisan passage in the U.S. Senate of the Marketplace Fairness Act went almost unnoticed.[6] In short, if we attend to those areas of commonality across difference, we can find ample grounds for unity.

The democratic sense of *justice*, which I have already introduced briefly, concerns *respect* for all people. All should be able and enabled to participate according to capacity and interest in the shared task of public leadership. There was a time when children with disabilities were institutionalized in large numbers. Today, we have learned and have had the courage to experiment with the better treatment of our children and with more respectful education for all people. My belated colleague, Dr. Maxine Harper, told her story of having to fight at every step of the way to pursue her education, when so many people believed that persons with severe cerebral palsy like hers were not meant for schooling. With loving parents and an irrepressible will, she eventually went so far as to earn her doctorate, a professorship in the University of Mississippi's School of Education, the directorship of our Center for Educational Research and Evaluation, and the respect of her colleagues. In the democratic period, the impediments to the life goals of people like Maxine must recede, and assumptions about superiority and inferiority must be rejected.[7] Not only are individuals harmed by injustice, but so too are society's interests set back. For when all people compete for public offices and in advocacy for guiding public endeavors, everyone is better off for having the largest pool of talent from which to draw and learn.

Each key term in my definition of democratic leadership is meant to adapt one of the virtues from Plato's *Republic* for the modern, democratic context as I have presented them to this point. *Respect* for the dignity of each person captures the meaning of justice in the democratic sense. *Experimentalism* connects especially with courage, but also with wisdom. *Inquiry* squarely relates to wisdom, but also to courage and guidance. Finally, the *common good* is a democratic adaptation of Plato's priority of unity, which is for him the target and motivation for moderation. What is common is more of a general idea, rather than universal. It is more appropriate as an ideal for free societies, since people ought to be free to think differently. At the same time, concern for problems felt in common has a moderating force that strengthens unity.

In sum, I call good leadership in general *judicious yet courageous guidance.* And given these explanations, I call desirable democratic leadership *respectful experimental inquiry for the common good.*

These virtues need to be guided by each other in order for good leadership to be achieved. Therefore, they are not meant to be considered entirely separately. While that is to be remembered, in the chapters that follow I will nevertheless emphasize these virtues one at a time, considering particular problems that Mississippi faces with respect to each point of guidance. All together, the problems I examine in the next chapters contribute in various ways to cultural and entrenched challenges that I have introduced in chapters 1 and 2.

4.

WISDOM DRAWN FROM INTELLIGENT PUBLIC INQUIRY

In the democratic context, wisdom should not be thought of as a property of only a select group, but as a matter of good public inquiry. Two examples of matters relevant for Mississippi bear examining in their connection to a culture of poverty and educational frustration. The first concerns culture in the schools, and the second is a set of related problems involving the lack of comprehensive sex education and the prevalence of teenage pregnancy. In each case, I argue that the wisest course of action has been clearly pointed out in the best public inquiry available and published. Despite what inquiry has shown, Mississippi's policies do not yet reflect some important insights for leadership.

In some ways, Mississippi retains a troubling and undemocratic orientation more than most other places in the United States. Nowhere is this trait more evident than in the permission given to the state's school administrators, who have the greatest freedom in the country to use corporal punishment in public schools. In his *Time* magazine article, "Why Is Paddling Still Allowed in Schools?" (2012), Adam Cohen writes, "In Mississippi, the No. 1 state for corporal punishment, 7.5 percent of students were physically disciplined."[1] Cohen explains that nineteen states presently allow corporal punishment despite the strong evidence showing the great harm it does. For an intense example, Mississippi's South Panola School District, with approximately 4,700 students, recorded 2,572 incidents of corporal punishment in the 2009–2010 school year.[2] A school year in Mississippi is 180 days, which translates to an average of slightly over 14 reported paddling incidents per school day, or once every 30 minutes in a 7-hour school day.

A former student of mine who is serving Mississippi through Teach for America explained to me her surprise upon witnessing corporal punishment. She said that it was perhaps the most startling experience she has witnessed in her time there. She reported to me that when parents were called about a child's poor behavior, parents would sometimes come to the school and beat their child on the school property. She was amazed and unnerved by the violence she witnessed and learned was tolerated. In fact, parents would sometimes recommend to the teachers that they strike the children when they misbehave.[3]

This anecdotal evidence confirms the studies which Cohen cites. He explains that "corporal punishment is not just a few raps on the knuckles with a ruler. It often means hitting a student on the bottom with a wooden paddle using considerable force. The mother of one [Texas girl] said that after her daughter was paddled, her bottom 'almost looked like it had been burned and blistered it was so bad.'"[4] If the idea motivating the use of corporal punishment is that it should enhance obedience and thereby behavior, consider that according to a 2006 *New York Times* article on the subject, "Nearly three quarters of all corporal punishment in the U.S. in 2002 took place in Texas, Arkansas, Mississippi, Tennessee, and Alabama."[5] None of these states is known for its educational success or greater obedience from students.[6]

If corporal punishment in schools only had little to no effect on improving performance and outcomes, that would be one thing, but in fact studies have shown that it does great harm. First, as Cohen reports,

> The case in favor of corporal punishment is remarkably thin. Supporters often invoke the injunction "Spare the rod, spoil the child," or simply point to the long tradition of paddling children and say they see no reason to stop now. But there is not a great deal of social-science evidence that paddling promotes better outcomes— and there is quite a bit that it does the reverse. Education experts say physical punishment instills a climate of fear in the classroom and is associated with students skipping class and dropping out of school.[7]

Beyond these general reports from experts, Cohen cites studies that show links to "mental health problems in children." He explains, "Studies have found that children who receive physical punishment are more likely to experience depression, suicide and antisocial behavior. A Canadian study published [in 2012] found a connection between corporal punishment and alcohol and drug abuse."[8] The consequences of corporal punishment are profoundly negative.

Demonstrating the danger of corporal punishment further, researchers Murray A. Straus and Emily M. Douglas, in their 2008 article titled, "Research on Spanking by Parents: Implications for Public Policy," the authors explain that

> There have been over a hundred studies, including longitudinal studies and experiments, concerning the effect of [corporal punishment (CP)] on children and adults. The meta analysis by Gershoff (2002) revealed 93 percent agreement on the harmful effects of CP. The

volume and the quality of the research have continued to grow since that publication. . . .

[Nevertheless, parents] continue to believe the cultural myth that spanking works when other methods do not. Given this belief, and given their concern for the well-being of children, it is not surprising that there is continued acceptance of the cultural myth that spanking may sometimes be necessary. . . . With over 90 percent agreement in the research showing that CP is a risk factor for development problems, we believe the evidence not only permits, but requires, a change in policy to one focused on ending CP.[9]

In addition, a 2012 national study released in *Pediatrics* has concluded that

it is important for pediatricians and other health care providers who work with children and parents to be aware of the link between physical punishment and mental disorders based on this study, which adds to the growing literature about the adverse outcomes associated with exposure to physical punishment. . . . From a public health perspective, reducing physical punishment may help to decrease the prevalence of mental disorders in the general population. Policies need to be focused on strategies to reduce physical punishment, which again points to the importance of positive parenting approaches.[10]

Democratic leadership will want what is best for children, guided by intelligent inquiry and scientific study. Traditional communities are wise to maintain those traditions that strengthen them and which produce virtue, but such communities should abandon those practices which promote vice or cause harm. In this case, corporal punishment only comes at a cost without benefit to Mississippi's children, families, and schools. Furthermore, as the experts have suggested, the environment for schools would be better if it were inviting, rather than punitive. The culture must shift if wise leadership is to bring about democratic progress based on the best available research.[11]

A potential challenge is worth considering. If parents in communities like South Panola want their kids to be disciplined physically in schools, would it not be democratic to do as the parents want? This concern has some weight intuitively, but there are two reasons to say no. The first is that mere popularity of a measure does not make it acceptable or democratic. It may be a popular idea to limit a person's free speech because people do not like him or her or a certain message. Nonetheless, democratic liberty for all requires the protection of the rights of minority groups and vulnerable populations. In a more extreme example, you cannot vote to make some citizens slaves and call that democratic. The principle to draw from these responses is that not all things that people and majorities might want are consistent with democratic respect for individuals, their rights, and most poignantly, their security of person. As I noted in a *Clarion Ledger* op-ed, included here as Appendix 7, the *Hall v. Tawney* (4th Cir. 1980) decision explained that excessive corporal punishment could be said to violate students' "right to ultimate bodily security, the most fundamental aspect of personal privacy, [which] is unmistakably established in our constitutional decisions as an attribute of the ordered liberty that is the concern of substantive due process." Even if it were a popular idea to perform corporal punishment on prisoners, the rules against cruel and unusual punishment would never allow it. People have rights, and among the most basic are rights to security of person, bodily safety. The state is charged with stemming abuse on the part of prison guards, but also of parents. Furthermore, it is charged in the schools with advancing the good of each student. Highly unhealthy lunches are considered a form of negligence to take proper care of students' dietary needs, for example.[12]

Democracy requires the development of each person's individuality and ability to grow into a free and equal citizen. Measures that hinder such development, even if they are popular, are undemocratic. Taking a further, extreme counterexample, consider a parent who abuses his or her child through clearly overstepped violence. I have in mind bloodying beatings that prompt widespread condemnation, such as one a professional athlete gave his child in 2014.[13] If a parent wanted that kind of discipline in the schools, we would surely say no. There are great differences in degree of severity of corporal punishment, yet the reason we would say no to the extreme case points to an important principle: schools are supposed to take proper care of students, making use of healthy means and practices that can help foster individual development. If practices are unhelpful or harmful, even simply in creating an unwelcoming and painful educational environment for students, beneficial and effective alternatives ought to be used instead. The point here is that democracy means more than popularity, even if popularity is often a way of selecting from acceptable options. The key is that the options selected do not infringe on people's rights or get in the way of the demands of democratic institutions.

On this point, I will conclude with advice from Plato and Dewey. If the idea of ending violent force in education seems modern, consider that Plato advocated against its use in education 2,400 years ago. In Book VII of the *Republic*, Plato wrote that "nothing taught by force stays in the soul."[14] Plato and Dewey offer both rational and moral arguments against corporal punishment, which can help us to understand the empirical evidence I have cited. Complementing Plato's lesson here, Dewey explains that violence is the frustration of ends and is different from forces which direct or redirect action without causing harm. We have to consider what kind of school culture makes the most sense for education, based on rational, moral, and empirical reasons. I would add here that just as I argued that economic growth is a consequence of moral growth, educational growth would also result from moral growth in ending corporal punishment, in selecting from the wisest practices available and studied. Furthermore, we can look to institutes and resources already available for insight, such as the Center for Effective Discipline.[15] Teaching young people to resolve their conflicts with reasoning and incentive systems diminishes the prison-like culture that the schools, such as in Meridian, Mississippi, have been said to embody.[16]

A second set of concerns could be targeted with greater wisdom drawn from the best available research, from the best public inquiry. These problems for Mississippi contribute to poverty, infant mortality, and educational frustration, such as dropout rates. I have in mind the lack of comprehensive sex education and a high incidence of teenage pregnancy. Comprehensive sex education would help alleviate some of the devastating effects of teenage pregnancy and sexually transmitted diseases.[17] Teenage pregnancy has been shown to lead fewer women to graduate from high school, for example.[18]

The science is clear on the effectiveness of comprehensive sex education and the general ineffectiveness of abstinence-only programs.[19] For instance, Norman A. Constantine writes in the *Journal of Adolescent Health* that

> Moral values do have a place in public policy discourse, yet it is imperative for all sides to recognize that there is no evidentiary basis for AO [abstinence-only] education and that a growing foundation of convergent evidence favors CSE [comprehensive sex education]. For sex education policy in the United States to become evidence-based, the overwhelming majority of parents and the general public who hold pragmatic public-health-oriented moral values about this issue will need to speak more assertively.[20]

In Mississippi, the common refrain is that teaching children about sex will increase sexual activity. The work of Pamela K. Kohler, Lisa Manhart, and William Lafferty has shown this to be false. They write that in fact, "Teaching about contraception was not associated with increased risk of adolescent sexual activity or STD. Adolescents who received comprehensive sex education had a lower risk of pregnancy than adolescents who received abstinence-only or no sex education."[21] The evidence could not be clearer that comprehensive sex education is the most effective way to keep the state's youth from sexually transmitted diseases and teenage pregnancy.

Two further related challenges are typically raised or assumed in resistance to comprehensive sex education. The first is a moral challenge to the instruction and the second is political. The moral challenge says that because sex engaged in outside of wedlock is wrong, it is a mistake to instruct young people in best practices for engaging in such immoral behavior. The political challenge argues that it is not the government's job or purview to teach sex education. Instead, it is the obligation of parents to teach young people about sex. Note that the political challenge does not necessarily have to agree with the moral challenge. There are parents who may wish to discourage young people from engaging in sex outside of wedlock, but themselves engaged in it and understand such behavior. My point in raising this qualification is that the political challenge does not hinge on the immorality of sex outside of wedlock.

The moral challenge to sex education is satisfied when sex education policies teach abstinence-only curricula. Hence, rather than advancing the political challenge, those who present the moral challenge do call for teaching sex education in school, so long as it presents sex as essentially unacceptable and to be abstained from prior to marriage. There are three ways in which the moral challenge is flawed, however, in its rejection of comprehensive sex education.

A first response builds on Kohler, Manhart, and Lafferty's findings that comprehensive sex education does not prompt increased sexual activity. The further point can be illustrated with an analogy. Speeding is dangerous and discouraged behavior, yet we reasonably teach people to buckle their seatbelts for greater safety. Teaching kids that increased safety results from wearing a seatbelt is not the same as encouraging speeding. People need the best tools available to make the smartest decisions for their own lives. Leaving young people ignorant does not match the need for greater wisdom.

A second response to the moral challenge would say that the belief that sex before marriage is immoral is itself a view not universally shared. Whatever the majority opinion, democracy calls for the protection of the rights of the minority.

It is certainly illegal to engage in statutory rape, sex involving adults and minors. When two minors engage in sexual behavior, however—a fifteen year old and a sixteen year old, for example—persons with different moral and religious points of view can reasonably disagree about whether they have done anything wrong. Therefore, the parents who do not see moral wrongdoing in young people's practice of safe sex are denied an appropriate school curriculum for their children by those who object morally to sex before wedlock.

A third response would say that policy can be designed to respect the parents who present the moral challenge, namely an opt-out policy for their children. This third response to the moral challenger also represents a key answer to the political challenger. The political challenger has essentially lost the debate when it comes to deciding between abstinence-only and more comprehensive sex education. Both approaches defy the political challenger. Nevertheless, if policy were drafted such that parents who present the political challenge could opt-out of having their children go through a sex education curriculum, or at least through the comprehensive version, their claim that government is imposing upon their own family would weaken. To appreciate the opt-out approach, it will help to consider the law that Mississippi has passed regarding sex education and how it failed to take up a possible way of maximally satisfying each of the various kinds of concerned parents.

Mississippi has been very slow to adopt policies reflecting the best available knowledge, drafting instead House Bill 999 in 2011, which forbids condom demonstrations, for example, and which lets school districts choose whether they will adopt an abstinence-only or abstinence-plus curriculum. The latter of these is more comprehensive, but not totally, given the law's limitation regarding condoms. One might think, according to these developments, that Mississippians do not want to follow the insights of the best available research. In fact, this is false. Mississippians have expressed their desire for change and for comprehensive sex education, but the state's officials have lacked the courage to act on the best evidence that science has offered. Of course, the people share some responsibility for electing such officials or for failing to speak up, especially when officials do not truly represent their will. In other words, it is not enough for specialists to discover the wisest solutions. People must also demand that their representatives exhibit the courage necessary to follow the guidance of wisdom, a topic I focus on in the next chapter. In the case of sex education, it is clear that the people want the policies that are best but public officials are getting in the way of progress.

As I explained in my 2012 piece in *Science Progress*[22]—which is included here as Appendix 4—a survey of 3,600 Mississippi parents revealed that 89.8 percent of respondents support education about birth control methods, which abstinence-only sex education excludes. Some school districts will choose abstinence-plus curricula for their children, but many have not and will not. As indicated by the title of the *Huffington Post*'s Reuters article (2012), "Mississippi Schools, With America's Highest Teen Pregnancy Rate, Largely Adopts [*sic*] Abstinence-Only Sex Education," state and school district leaders are choosing a sex education curriculum which is neither the most effective form nor the one that the vast majority of Mississippians want.[23] Even though Mississippians wish to fight teenage pregnancy, sexually transmitted diseases, and causes of dropout and poverty, representatives at the state and district levels are failing to make the wise choice. They are not reflecting the views of their constituents, which, as I have said, is also a sign that citizens ought to act and vote accordingly. This latter point is a good example of how crucial it is for leadership to be understood democratically—it is not all up to public officials. Citizens also bear important responsibilities.

The case of sex education represents an instance of what Plato would call a conflicted soul, in which spirited devotion to traditions overpowers the intellect. If that is right, then the people will say that they want what is best, yet continue to elect officials or to fail to turn out to vote, resulting in policymaking that runs counter to wise leadership. It is unfair to blame only political representatives regarding the issue of sex education. Citizens must stand up to offer judicious yet courageous guidance, demanding that representatives choose what the best public inquiry recommends. After all, if the issue is that some people wish that their children not be provided comprehensive sex education in places that adopt it, the solution is straightforward: parental consent forms with opt-out opportunities. With that kind of arrangement, families who want their children educated comprehensively about sex can get what they want and so can those who object to it for their children. At present, Mississippi school districts that choose an abstinence-only curriculum offer no options for parents who want more comprehensive sex education for their children. Instead, a comprehensive curriculum in all schools, complemented with an opt-out opportunity for parents who want their kids to have an abstinence-only curriculum, is the solution that more wisely offers all what they need and accept for their own children.

The problems of corporal punishment and sex education in Mississippi are clear examples of opportunities for greater wisdom, courage, and democratic respect for all Mississippians. Both of these problems are rooted in a culture that fails to respect all children as human beings. This mistake shows a lack of wisdom and of justice. Ultimately, we cannot teach children respect if we do not respect them in the first place. In addition, division and disrespect for real problems misdirect politicians into crafting the wrong policies and legislation. Recall that for Plato, courage involves fearing the right things and not fearing the wrong things. For Dewey, courage calls us to think critically and to be ready for the challenges of public communication, engagement, and action. Therefore, it is vital for democratic leadership to exhibit the courage necessary to pursue what wisdom demands. Given this need to enable the will to bring about change, I turn next to the virtue of courage.

5.

COURAGE FOR
EXPERIMENTAL INQUIRY
AND ACTION

While each virtue of good leadership has its own characteristics, each of the virtues must be guided by the others.
Courage depends on the wise guidance of one's spirit. Spirit
moved without wisdom and justice can lead to hatred and
division. At the same time, it takes courage to bring practices in line with what wisdom teaches us through the processes of democratic inquiry. When thinking about the nature
of courage in the democratic context, and specifically with
respect to the challenges and opportunities for Mississippi's
progress, it is evident in the need to experiment.

Courage through experimentalism can help Mississippi
in many areas. In chapter 2, I noted one example of ways in
which the state can experiment with new practices in education, such as has been done in some successful charter
school ventures. The important part, as I noted in chapter 2,
is the will to experiment, not necessarily the use of charter
schools as the mechanism for our experiments. Recall that
courage means fearing the right things and not the wrong
things, according to Plato, such as in working to change the
culture of racism that lingers in the state, the second example and challenge that I will consider in this chapter. At the
University of Mississippi, it took courage for student leaders to experiment with resistance to the traditions that have

held Mississippi back. My experience in Oxford, Mississippi, motivates my focus on examples here, though problems and progress are to be found in many areas around the state. I have had the good fortune to watch brave students fight for the crucial values central to the success of educational institutions. They have and are cause to be proud of Mississippi and its young people.

With regard to charter schools, I have mentioned the remarkable success of the KIPP Delta schools just on the other side of the Mississippi River. KIPP has its critics, who most importantly point to the challenge of achieving the KIPP level successes on a large scale.[1] As I write this chapter, there are currently no KIPP schools in Mississippi, given that they first had to be legally permitted, something that a 2013 law has only recently made possible. The proposals for reform that have been most successful in Mississippi call for permitting failing schools to be converted into public charter schools, not for presently successful schools to follow a charter school model. Despite popular confusion on the subject, charter schools are *public* schools. People associate them with voucher programs, but the latter are systems whereby funds for a public school student's education are transferred to a private school to offset costs for parents. Charter schools, by contrast, are simply public schools directed by a charter approved in one of a variety of ways according to what is required for charters in state legislation. They are typically freed from a number of constraints on traditional public schools in exchange for high expectations of improved performance. Among the differences, for example, is the fact that charter schools can often hire a greater variety of possible teachers, circumventing some certification requirements. They can also stay open for longer days and are accorded greater operational autonomy in general.

To have their charters renewed, they must show evidence of strong student performance and results.[2]

Democratic Party officeholders and supporters are sometimes opposed to charter schools because of the force of teachers' unions or advocacy groups, which typically support Democrats. Those unions or groups are concerned about the ways in which charter schools might loosen the requirements for school districts to support their teachers or to protect their job security. Republicans tend to favor charter schools as an option for introducing competition and choice into the public school process but sometimes resist them because of the potential to take funds away from successful public schools. As a result, the Mississippi legislature has tried several times over the years but only in the last few years passed charter school legislation.[3]

In an essay in the *Clarion Ledger* included here as Appendix 6, I have advocated for giving charters a try, particularly where schools are failing.[4] This limitation would avoid the problem of tampering with successful schools. At the same time, it would offer communities with failing schools the chance to try a new tack for educating their kids. To be sure, it will take courage to experiment. Some who resist setting up charter schools suggest that if a solution will work in charter schools, why not apply that solution to all schools? This is an interesting question, but it fails to consider the fact that charter schools are experiments to see what works. In other words, simply making a school a charter does nothing to guarantee its success. In fact, in some states, such as Arizona, charters underperform in comparison with their traditional counterparts.[5] Ultimately, it takes courage to try a new experiment and to keep an open mind. It is unrealistic to think that one can easily determine in advance some simple formula that will address problems in an overarching way without careful study and trial and error. People aiming to offer judicious yet courageous guidance must see themselves as part of an experiment and as capable of learning and being convinced. Experiments also typically require repetitions and refinements, upon learning from initial trials.

Critics of the charter schools movement are sometimes concerned about the students who are left behind in traditional schools when stronger students move to charters. Any experiment, however, can be said to have such an effect temporarily. Take drug trials as an illustration. When you test to see whether innovations, such as new medicines or new educational methods or circumstances make a difference, you have to differentiate the experimental group from a control group. The control group does not get the newly developed treatment, so that we can see whether there is a real difference between people conventionally treated and those in the experimental group.

Of course, when it comes to schools, experiments are not perfectly scientific. The people who self-select or who seek out charter school opportunities may share characteristics that differentiate those students from students in the traditional school, whose parents may be less involved. This is one of the challenges that critics of charter schools raise. After all, if you simply select the best students out of traditional schools, we should not be too surprised when average performance is higher. That intuition diminishes the strength of the argument we can make about the results of charter schools experiments. While this is true, there are two features of this challenge that can be answered. First, if parental involvement is evidently part of the success of charter school students—if we can show that this is part of what makes them more successful—then we can design policy and implement institutional mechanisms aimed at increasing parental involvement in education for kids who are at risk,[6] educationally speaking.

The second point to make is that charter schools, when understood as experiments, are not meant to keep insights developed in them to themselves alone. The point of learning from experiments would be in part to see what will work for the sake of sharing and spreading successful innovations. Thus, when I agree to participate in a double-blind study, I understand that I may be placed in the control group or in the experimental group. I may hope to be treated with the experimental drug, but if we are to learn, we must experiment, trying different, new ideas in new places. New ideas, however, tend to be feared, since we do not know how well or poorly they will work. The fear we might have of failure in educational innovations might lead people to avoid experimentation. Given this troubling feature of widespread experimentation, it is normal and wisest to experiment only on a small sample at first, trying elsewhere and more widely after tested and refined results. Thus, the fact of testing educational experiments in innovation on select groups is the best way to avoid more widespread failure. This in turn diminishes fear in experimentation and hence enhances our courage to try. For all of these reasons, whether we decide to test out experiments in educational innovations within the Department of Education or through a charter process—overseen by the state as well—wise leadership ought also to be courageous in trying out new ways to help young people succeed in school.

Aside from charter schools, experimentation and courage are also needed in the area of race relations. As I will argue in the next chapter, Mississippi has a lot of work to do to achieve greater unity as a state. I believe that Plato was right in the passage highlighted in the epigraph opening this book, where he warns that whatever tears a city apart is among the greatest evils. To confront such evils, however, takes a deep and uncommon courage. One expects such courage to come from those who are older and more experienced, who know better than younger people what to fear and what not to fear. My examples of courage, however, come from college students, and I believe that Mississippi needs and will benefit from more and more young people like the ones I will describe. In a generation, these students will be public figures and continue to contribute to respectful experimental inquiry for the common good, working to reconstruct Mississippi's culture.

In 2009, Artair Rogers was elected president of the Associated Student Body of the University of Mississippi. He was only the second African American student to have won the office. As his tenure began, he quickly sought to tackle the issue of a chant that was being yelled at the end of the school band's performance of "From Dixie with Love" at football games. The song is a creative medley of "Dixie" and "Battle Hymn of the Republic." The idea behind the medley, I surmised, was to bring North and South together and to move forward. Unfortunately, at the end of the song, the concluding cadence led into a chant started around 2005, in which students, alumni, and others yelled, "The South will rise again!"

The chant was troubling for many. Even when people explained that they wanted to reclaim the phrase, many others felt unwelcome and insulted by it. Given Rogers's prompting, echoed by members of a student group called One Mississippi, the new chancellor, Dan Jones, agreed to request that the crowds stop yelling the chant. He explained that in the event that they continue, he would have the band change its song roster, removing the medley that prompted the chant. When the crowd continued as usual, the chancellor followed through on his promise and drew much anger and criticism. Artair, members of One Mississippi, and the chancellor exhibited courage and a willingness to try a new way of pursuing unity, rejecting the outdated symbols of the past. In November 2009, after much discussion on the controversy about the song and the chant, the Ku Klux Klan announced that it was coming to protest the chancellor's decision.

Eleven members of the Klan came in full regalia to protest the university's decision, drawing national press. With only a few days warning, the students of One Mississippi led an effort to fight the negative culture that the Klan represents and to assert the values for which the university stands today. While most of the headlines were the kinds you do not want describing your university, one in particular caught the scene. According to the Associated Press (AP) on the *Huffington Post*, "KKK Rally at Ole Miss: Klan Outnumbered by Protestors," "AP estimated that 250 people showed up to protest the Klan's presence."[7] In addition, given the leadership of students like Artair and a number of other great students, "The real story of the day" came together. The AP wrote,

> The real story of the day was the students, faculty, staff and alumni who gathered peacefully and read the University's creed in unison repeatedly a few hundred feet from where the Klan had gathered. Organized by One Mississippi, a student group working towards greater social integration at Ole Miss, protesters wore shirts that said "TURN YOUR BACK ON HATE . . . (I live by the UM Creed)" and stickers with one simple word: "Unity." Before and after the rally, they talked to fans

in town for the game about their message and plan to make their way through the ten-acre, park-like Grove, passing out copies of the UM creed to fans.[8]

These students had the courage required to face one of the clearest symbols of hatred and disunity still surviving today, the Ku Klux Klan. Consider that among the central forces the Klan sought to motivate was fear.[9]

A key difference between Plato and Dewey, between authoritarianism and democracy, concerns the freedom of communication. In a free and democratic society, communication must be maximally free. Very few limits are allowed, such as on speech that significantly harms others, as in cases of libel or yelling "fire" in a theater. Protection of the freedom of thought and expression is vital for the democratic pursuit of wisdom, and it also requires significant courage. In this respect, Dewey and contemporary public philosopher Cornel West find communication and critical thinking to be immensely powerful, important, and at times frightening. For a simple example of the fear people experience, consider that in a March 2001 Gallup poll, public speaking was the second greatest fear Americans admitted, following only snakes.[10] While public speaking makes people nervous and afraid, speaking out against hate groups and putting oneself in the public eye—to proclaim values and challenge others' ideas, and especially our friends'—demands a great deal more courage.

Since the incident of the Klan's visit, a number of students have demonstrated remarkable courage in combating hateful and unpleasant messages. Another example comes from my experience at the University of Mississippi, though again, I emphasize that developments such as these can and do take place around the state.

Having witnessed racism behind closed doors at a fraternity meeting during the pledge decision procedure in the 2010–2011 school year, University of Mississippi student Hunter Nicholson was disgusted. He took some time to meet with other students in the Greek system to see how widespread this kind of interaction was. He drafted a thoughtful and profoundly challenging statement about "Race and the Greek System at Ole Miss," which he published in the *Daily Mississippian*, the University of Mississippi's student newspaper. Telling his story and reporting on his findings from friends in the Greek system, Hunter argued that "the racial discrimination going on in our Greek system must stop."[11] He lost a few friends by speaking out, but he was also troubled that they thought that the way things were done was acceptable, he told me.

Another student, Lexi Thoman, contributed a piece to the student newspaper at the University of Mississippi in an effort to reshape the campus culture. In "The Ghosts of Ole Miss Are Far from Dead," Thoman expressed her shock at the disturbance that arose on campus the night of the presidential election of 2012. Freshmen living on campus had come together and chanted the name of their favored candidate. When President Obama won a second term, some unhappy students collected Obama/Biden yard signs, and a few students lit a sign on fire. White and black students variously expressed anger and happiness close to one another and soon epithets were exclaimed and disorder broke out.

Very little violence took place that night. Records noted that a woman slapped a man and a plastic soda bottle was thrown at a passing car. Yet the symbolic violence and destruction of yard signs caught attention.[12] As Thoman pointed out in her piece, however, these events occurred in the fiftieth anniversary year of the enrollment of James Meredith at the University of Mississippi, who integrated the university as the first African American student. Thoman writes, "The protestors have reminded the entire nation of the stereotype that Ole Miss has fought for fifty years to dispel. They perpetuated the belief that we are racist, that we are ignorant and that we are unwilling to accept inevitable social change."[13] In a rich example of the exercise of democratic leadership and with special courage, she calls her fellow students to embody the values of the university's creed. That statement expresses belief in fairness and civility and in the need to respect the dignity of each person. It is worth noting here that the university's creed echoes Dewey's understanding of justice, which I touched on very briefly in chapter 3, concerning the dignity and worth of each person, and hence embodies central democratic values. "What happens now is up to us," Thoman writes. "The ghosts of Ole Miss might not be dead, but we can refuse to be defined by them."[14]

The night after the disturbance in 2012, about 700 students, faculty, and staff gathered for a candlelight vigil, calling for racial harmony and unity on campus. The cover of this book was taken that night. With demonstrations like these and the examples of courageous young moral leaders, students have challenged each other and fellow citizens to live more virtuously, wisely, moderately, and respectfully. It takes a great deal of courage to speak out and to experiment in leadership for the reconstruction of Mississippi's culture. At the same time, it is worth noting that institutional statements of value, like the university's creed, can be remarkably useful in pointing to important, shared values. Courageous people can draw from such institutional and cultural resources as they challenge others to join together in the fulfillment of virtuous practices and aims.

6.

MODERATION, UNITY, AND
THE COMMON GOOD

The mutually important virtues cannot totally be isolated from one another, which is why moderation has come up several times in the preceding chapters. In emphasizing it especially in this chapter, some vital facets of this virtue and its processes and products can be clarified. Moderation, unity, and commonality are related guides for leadership that are crucial both in Plato's *Republic* and in Dewey's and modern democratic thinkers' conceptions of the public good. Plato suggests that moderation, in the pursuit of unity, is among the most important virtues for the good society. If a society is not one, how can it work together courageously, guided by wisdom and justice? The sports team made up of strong players—my stand-in for wisdom in this analogy—and in which each player is spirited and ready to work hard will nevertheless make a poor team if the players do not work together, playing as one. Applying this insight to the city, Plato asked, "Is there any greater evil we can mention for a city than that which tears it apart and makes it many instead of one? Or any greater good than that which binds it together and makes it one?"[1] In this guiding virtue, furthermore, we see why Plato was wary of democracy. In democratic societies, liberty is prized above all. When people act freely, without rulers, they can easily find themselves lacking in unity of purpose. If this is true, cities will split and internal warring will break out. The danger that Plato has in mind, however, does not require authoritarian thinking to recognize and address, according to Dewey.

Plato's warning of civil war was neither far from the truth nor difficult to relate to democratic societies. Indeed, in the United States, a civil war and dissolution of the union was in the early days greatly feared even by the eventual commander of the Confederate forces, Robert E. Lee, who earlier had been a colonel in the US Army. After expressing his disapproval of the North's actions against the South, Lee nevertheless summed up his concern as an American about the potential for war in an 1861 letter to G. W. P. Custis. Lee wrote,

> As an American citizen, I take great pride in my country, her prosperity and institutions, and would defend any State if her rights were invaded. But I can anticipate no greater calamity for the country than a dissolution of the Union. It would be an accumulation of all the evils we complain of, and I am willing to sacrifice everything but honor for its preservation.[2] I hope, therefore, that all constitutional means will be exhausted before there is a resort to force. Secession is nothing but revolution. The framers of our Constitution never exhausted so much labor, wisdom and forbearance in its formation, and surrounded it with so many guards and securities, if it was intended to be broken by every member of the Confederacy at will. It is intended for "perpetual union," so expressed in the preamble, and for the establishment of a government, not a compact, which can only be dissolved by revolution, or the consent of all the people in convention assembled. It is idle to talk of secession. Anarchy would have been

established, and not a government, by Washington, Hamilton, Jefferson, Madison, and the other patriots of the Revolution.[3]

In this extended passage, we can see two things important for understanding Plato, Dewey, as well as American and other modern democracies today. The first point is to note the vital importance of unity, even if not of the kind which totalitarians like Plato might enforce. Instead, harmony across difference is the virtue to be strived for through the embodiment of democratic moderation.

The second point is the inevitable overlap of multiple identities that will arise in any large society. In this sense, the further worry Plato warned against must again be noted. At the beginning of this book, I included a second passage from Plato's *Republic* which is especially helpful here. Plato wrote that "we'll have to find a greater title for [larger cities] because each of them is a great many cities, not *a* city. . . . At any rate, each of them consists of two cities at war with one another, that of the poor and that of the rich, and that each of these contains a great many."[4] The larger a society, it seems, the more difficult it will be to achieve unity. As I have said, in the democratic age, a better term for appreciating Platonic unity is the term *commonality*, such as in the "common good." The reason for this is that the concept of what is common points to overlapping identity despite difference. Therefore, in large societies, the goal cannot be perfect unity, given how much difference is found among the people. At the same time, some commonalities can be noted and embraced for the sake of unifying a people in limited or temporary ways.

Whether we use the plural "these United States" or "the

United States" in the singular, more common today, the nation is explicitly in name an attempt to achieve a unity of smaller communities. The founders recognized that it was important to let local communities decide a great deal of their laws and to restrict the larger, federal government to matters which concern the overlapping and common interests of the many states. This was the intention behind the Tenth Amendment to the US Constitution.[5] When it comes to Mississippi, and to the virtue of moderation, unity, or common good among Mississippians, we find quite a difficult case of overlapping identities to consider.

Mississippians are divided in many ways: between the rich and the poor, the white and the black, the educated and the uneducated, and the supporter of state control and of federal control. Key indicators of division are observable in forms of self-segregation, as in schools and in churches. The solution to such problems is not simple, yet areas of commonality can be noted and used for the sake of making people care more about each other, and thus fight for the common good of all.

A remarkable first place to recognize disunity and a separation of the people that tears them apart can be noted in the exponential growth of private white academies in Mississippi which occurred at the time when school integration was imposed on Mississippi by the federal government. Between 1966 and 1974, the number of students enrolled in private academies jumped from roughly 3,000 to nearly 45,000. In his careful analysis, "Movement-Countermovement Dynamics and the Emergence of New Institutions: The Case of 'White Flight' Schools in Mississippi" (2002), author Kenneth T. Andrews argues that "[the] establishment of academies was a countermovement strategy that flowed out of the prior history of organized white resistance to the civil-rights movement. In other words, whites were not only responding to court intervention and the proportion of African Americans in their community, but to the social movement mobilization of that community."[6] In other parts of the United States that resisted integration, some conflicts took the form of the redrawing school district boundaries. In Mississippi, however, a very rural state where the population is little consolidated, many communities could not support multiple public schools. Therefore, private academies were founded to address the demand.

Mississippi is not unique in seeing many public schools enroll nearly all black students. Urban centers around the country have seen white flight to suburbs.[7] In addition, it is not evident how integration efforts should be evaluated, according to debates that have been long-standing in the study of race. For instance, Elizabeth Anderson's book, *The Imperative of Integration* (2010), begins with her shock at the white self-segregation that she witnessed in Michigan.[8] She believes that integration is a moral imperative, even though so many have abandoned it despite its having been a central goal of the civil rights movement. All the various methods of addressing the gaps between the advantages of white citizens and the correlative disadvantages for black citizens, she argues, will be unsuccessful without integration. She believes that racial segregation is a fundamental cause of racial injustice. At the same time, former Harvard professor of law Derrick Bell argued that it is a mistake to see *Brown v. Board of Education* (1954) as a success. Bell has questioned the feasibility of successful and meaningful integration. He has argued that "the interests of blacks in quality education might now be better served by concentration on improving the quality of existing schools, whether desegregated or not."[9] Bell explains that "successful magnet schools may provide a lesson that effective schools for blacks must be a primary goal rather than a secondary result of integration."[10]

As Bell suggests and the KIPP Delta schools demonstrate, excellent schools can help open opportunities for poor and African American students, even if they are not significantly integrated. While I agree with Bell that quality education ought to be a priority, the unity required for motivating people to fight for quality education for all, rather than for their own children only, may well depend on at least significant interaction, if not integration, as Anderson argues. My point here is not to pretend that there is a simple solution to the questions these scholars raise. At the same time, the vital need for unity in Mississippi calls for asking about how people can come to feel that others' successes and failures, benefits and threats, are to be treated as their own.

For one thing, greater education about economics could be of help. One form of self-interested unity[11] would come when more people understand that the "rising tide lifts all boats"[12]—that all will have greater economic success when more people have means to engage in commerce.[13] The idea here is not Benjamin Friedman's, discussed in chapter 1, that growth will render greater moral consideration, but rather that growth *for all* as a *moral* aspiration is mutually helpful. Somehow, people must come to care about each other in the first place. Anderson believes that it is interaction brought about through integration that will help us to achieve such results. And though some, like Bell, will be skeptical, Anderson suggests in a précis about her book that "we should not foreclose hope. After all, only a few years ago the idea of a black president was regarded by many Americans to be an unrealizable dream."[14]

In the *Republic*, Plato suggests that rulers should tell a "noble lie" to unify people, to achieve unity across difference. The lie he proposed was intended to motivate people to take up arms in defense of their neighbors, to feel injured when others are injured, and therefore to come to the aid of others when they suffer. Today, Deweyans, Americans, and Mississippians have truth and beliefs to draw on, no longer needing Plato's falsehoods. For Dewey, democratic ends must be pursued with democratic means. Leadership through deception can only be considered authoritarian rather than democratic. Many Americans and a high percentage of Mississippians, furthermore, are strong believers in religious scriptures, which consider a unifying ideal to be God's truth, not a lie. Jane Dailey notes the force of unity that Christianity represents in her article "Sex, Segregation, and the Sacred after *Brown*" (2004).[15] Dailey relates Martin Luther King Jr.'s religious condemnation of segregation. She writes,

> "The Church is first of all the body of Christ, and in that Body we are one, not races or clans," declared another white Mississippi Methodist minister. King agreed: The "church is the Body of Christ. So when the church is true to its nature it knows neither division nor disunity. I am disturbed about what you [segregationists] are doing to the Body of Christ." The "beloved community," as King explained on another occasion, had to be integrated because "segregation is a blatant denial of the unity which we all have in Jesus Christ."[16]

It seems plausible, given these outlooks, to imagine a strong religious movement to bring people together in a state which the *Christian Post* (Washington, DC) has named the "nation's 'most religious' population."[17]

Even in church, however, Mississippians are divided

and suffer from what Plato called the greatest evil for the state—disunity.[18] According to a *CNN* writer, "Nine out of ten congregations in the U.S. are segregated."[19] Furthermore, even where some churches have made initial steps to be inclusive, Mississippi has found ways to shock the world with its intransigence. *The Guardian* of London reported in 2012 on the story of Charles and Te'Andrea Wilson, an African American couple who were to be married in their majority white church. Author Ed Pilkington writes, "God's love is colour blind. Not, it seems, when it comes to the First Baptist church of Crystal Springs in Mississippi."[20] The Wilsons, who had been attending the church for months and had planned to be wed there, were forbidden from marrying in the church. The pastor "told a TV station weddings of black couples had never happened in the church," Pilkington reports, and according to members of the congregation, "It was just not going to happen." Church members threatened to vote out the pastor if he married them there. Pilkington continues, "'When I got the news I couldn't believe it at first,' Charles Wilson told the Jackson *Clarion Ledger*. 'This is not a matter of colour for me, it's about God, and what better place to get married than God's sanctuary. God's love is colour blind.'"[21] It seems, then, that when it comes to race, even guiding beliefs held dear among the most religious people in the nation sometimes are not strong enough forces for unity in Mississippi, at least so far.[22]

Even though stories like the Wilsons' here inspire disbelief and reason to be skeptical about unity in Mississippi, when considered in the big picture, perhaps there is still cause for hope. The First Baptist Church of Crystal Springs promptly apologized to the Wilsons and to the world. Their apology need not satisfy the Wilsons, but it does demonstrate the shame that resulted when the world judged the Crys-

tal Springs church's prejudice. When Londoners and New
Zealanders, not to mention Tennesseans and Iowans, read
once again about Mississippi racism, the children of Mississippians suffer. Their job prospects and the value of their
diplomas are affected by an identity that the vast majority of
graduates wish to shed. Still, initial steps toward such caring
are suggested in the shaming that was due to the offending
church, for instance, whose hypocrisy in proclaiming Christian values while discriminating against church members is
difficult to stomach.[23]

Despite some failings, which can occur in any group or
endeavor, religious experience can be a vital force for estab-
lishing common ground across difference. Dewey's *A Common Faith* (1934) argued that while religions divide people,
all experience exhibits what he called a religious dimension,
which can inspire unity.[24] By this, he meant the experience
of value, inescapable in life, which suggests in any given situation a spectrum of better and worse conditions. That spectrum implies an ideal of perfection, even if we cannot con-
ceive of it concretely. The experience of that continuum of
better and worse, which implies a direction toward perfection, captures what Dewey called the divine. The point here
is that Dewey offered a way of thinking about the religious
aspects of experience in order to unify people, to bring them
together.

The problem is that in so many instances, religion is used
for the opposite of moderation or unity. It is too often instead
a cause for division, discrimination, even hatred. In Mississippi and elsewhere, religion is sometimes used to motivate
resistance to the intellect, as in the scriptural forces prompting people to want to exclude sex education and good science education from schools.[25] It is true that philosophers
and intellectuals have at times been great challengers to re-

ligion, both in isolating particular practices as wrong—such as some of the examples I have mentioned—and in opposing any or all religion, as in the case of philosophical atheists or agnostics.[26] But at the same time, others like Dewey have sought ways to highlight what is invaluable about religious experience for drawing people together.[27] Following in Dewey's footsteps, contemporary philosopher Cornel West has been a strong and consistent—and hence radical—Christian, one who shares Dewey's goal of unity.[28]

West's influential book, *Prophecy Deliverance! An Afro-American Revolutionary Christianity* (1982), laid the foundation for much of his later thinking and political activism. In his efforts, West seeks not division but unity. A Christian and intellectual leader, West writes in his more recent and popular book, *Hope on a Tightrope* (2008),

> Martin Luther King, Jr., following the great Benjamin
> E. Mays, used to say we are all part of one garment
> of destiny, one inextricable network of mutuality. We
> have to acknowledge that, whether we like each other
> or not. Traditionally, black people have labored under
> the false notion that we must be homogeneous to be
> strong. They confused homogeneity with unity. Strong
> unity actually comes from affirming our diversity.[29]

While certainly a provocative figure, West demonstrates how one can be a strong Christian, an intellectual, and an advocate for the poor. West sees in intellectually guided and courageous faith the will to resist blind or mean beliefs supported with Scripture. He suggests reasons for courage, hope, and faith in the democratic potential of philosophical wisdom, justice, unity, and leadership. In these efforts, West has been in many ways a great champion of Dewey's democratic ideals and philosophy.

In my own experience, I have seen some of the greater signs of hope, particularly in talented college students. Some of my black students' parents at first felt uncomfortable sending their children to the University of Mississippi, students have told me, but these young people very much wanted to come—I present some examples in Appendix 2. The younger generation will have an education in the same professional institution that educates the white political officials of the state. Students of all backgrounds want to change Mississippi. They have inspired me to hope for the unity necessary to tackle Mississippi's deep and long-standing problems. They might lead in religious organizations, in student groups, in their journalistic writings, and in their eventual careers and public service. They will be enabled wherever our institutions make virtuous, democratic values explicit, such as in the University of Mississippi's creed. The unity that is possible and promising, furthermore, is vital for pursuing the remaining virtue and the subject of chapter 7, namely justice.

7.

JUSTICE AS RESPECT
FOR THE DIGNITY AND
WORTH OF ALL

While justice is the virtue that Plato describes last in the *Republic*, understanding it was the central purpose that prompted him to think about all four of the virtues. Plato thought that justice involves having each part or group in society do that which is its function. His idea of what is the task of each part of a whole works well when we consider sailors on a ship, each assigned a role, but it works poorly when applied to classes of people in blanket fashion. Even while Plato admitted that in rare cases a person born of parents who both have "bronze" character could in fact turn out to fit in a higher or more valuable group, the very idea of thinking about such categories is unnerving today to the democratic citizen, and Dewey took the rejection of this idea to be a centerpiece of democratic thinking. Nevertheless, Mississippi has retained such an outdated way of thinking, applying it unjustly to minority and poor citizens. This is evident in several ways. First, the continued segregation of citizens in their private white academies and black public schools separates groups, and these groups reap significantly different results in educational evaluations. Second and related to the first point, disadvantaged citizens in the state thereby become tracked into a limited set of avenues and life possibilities. Third, the culture in Mississippi tolerates these inequities, even when they result in incredible differences in rates of incarceration, and even as they inspire citizens to discriminate unjustifiably in ways that are hurtful and deadly.

One might think that the private academies I have mentioned divided people only in the early stages of forced integration of the public schools. One would be wrong. In December 2012, Sarah Carr published an essay in *The Atlantic* describing the continuing practices of self-segregation in Mississippi. In her article, "In Southern Towns, 'Segregation Academies' Are Still Going Strong," Carr writes that

> [more] than four decades after they were established, "segregation academies" in Mississippi towns like Indianola continue to define nearly every aspect of community life. Hundreds of these schools opened across the country in the twenty years after the *Brown v. Board* decision, particularly in southern states like Mississippi, Arkansas, Alabama, and Virginia. While an unknown number endure outside of Mississippi, the Delta remains their strongest bastion.[1]

If people were simply seeking the best schools for their children, it still would not explain the incredibly low percentage of African American students in the private academy schools. In the Mississippi Delta, Carr explains, there are approximately thirty-five academies whose enrollment is 98 percent white, or higher. At the same time, the majority of these segregated academies are not high-performing schools. Carr reports that former Mississippi secretary of state "Dick Molpus [has] added that Mississippi towns have limited amounts of money, power, and influence. 'When those three things are divided between black public schools and white academies, both offer substandard education," he said."[2]

Carr also interviewed one of the first African Americans to integrate the public schools in Indianola, Mississippi, Mr. Hury Minniefield. He predicts that the schools that are self-segregated today will never integrate. As Carr reports, Minniefield suggested that "it has not been achieved and it will likely never be achieved. It's because of the mental resistance of Caucasians against integrating with blacks. . . . Until the white race can see their former slaves as equals, it will not happen. [So] the white community would prefer not to pay a dime to the [nearly all black] public schools. . . . It's had a devastating effect on resources and the upward mobility of the community."[3] Minniefield here notes the fact that when upward mobility is inhibited for the African American population in Indianola, the community's mobility is impeded as well.

Indianola's white mayor, Steve Rosenthal, claims that the white community would not avoid the public schools if they were of proper quality. He told Carr that "if there's mistrust, it's the black community towards the whites."[4] In this context, we see how even small towns can come to be divided so thoroughly, blaming one another and warring with one another, metaphorically speaking, just in the way that Plato imagined. When we develop great differences in wealth and poverty, or if we get large cities, they cannot rightly be called *a* city, but many. They are at war with themselves and thereby undermine their own potential. Those who are best at a job are deselected because of irrelevancies like race. People who should care for one another if the community is to thrive, and who even share deeply held beliefs about a deity who is their common father, are bitterly divided and suffering. The condition of such cities and societies cannot be called anything but vicious, rather than virtuous, and a home to profound injustice.

In today's language, we often think about justice or injustice in a local or interactional way. A victim of injustice is said to be harmed particularly or directly, in most cases. In Plato's day, but also in our modern and democratic reinterpretation, we can consider the justice of a community or society. We can ask whether each part of a group is doing that at which it is best, or we can ask, as Dewey and James Tufts would, whether social action is guided by an appreciation of the worth and dignity of each person, their democratic understanding of justice. In the former case, the only way for a person to say that societies like the one Carr describes in Indianola, Mississippi, are just is to assume that African Americans are where they should be, serving in roles tied to poverty and incarceration. To think this, however, is to embody the most thoroughgoing racism, white supremacy, and disrespect for the dignity and worth of each person. Those who reject the racist belief that talent is unevenly distributed between blacks and whites should find it unacceptable that white students in the state score on average four points higher on the ACT's college preparatory exam than black students.[5] In addition, anyone who rejects racism should find deeply troubling the fact that while only 36 percent of Mississippians are African Americans, they make up 61 percent of persons who are incarcerated.[6]

There are philosophers like Robert Nozick who have thought that justice is not to be found at the level of patterns. Rather, Nozick believed that justice is a matter found at the level of individual interactions, such as when two people contract with one another and follow through on the deal.[7] Injustice occurs in unfair dealing at the transactional level, he claimed. The problem with Nozick's view, however, is that the forces of racism and division are ubiquitous and so deeply engrained that they no longer need explicit policies or enforcement. Alternate methods have been devised that avoid explicit statements. Now racism is conveyed in tacit ways, such as in the foolish self-fulfilling prophecy whereby people choose not to fund public schools because they are inadequate for their children.[8] If there were no private schools in Mississippi, were they to be made illegal tomorrow, the level of funding for public schools in Mississippi would rise steeply, I believe. Advantaged citizens would not tolerate inadequate public schools for their own children. Nozick's point for our present case is irrelevant. For what he is explaining is that some patterns can arise without anyone intending them to occur. How can people be blamed for something that no one individual planned to make happen? In such cases, a pattern arose only by chance. For one answer, those offering judicious yet courageous guidance ought to consider the potential result of many people acting freely, such as when there is a run on the banks, or when people in a crowd panic and flee, injuring and killing young children.[9]

Recognizing the potential dangers of the patterns of free individual action, people engaged in respectful experimental inquiry for the common good ought to direct fellow citizens and politicians to be cautious, to follow the guidance of wisdom and justice. While we do sometimes forgive people for the consequences of their actions that they could not have intended or which they could not have avoided, the case is different in Mississippi. It is clear and has been explicitly the intention of people to subjugate others, to treat them as less important, and to separate from them in order for the powerful to maintain their superiority. The defeat and removal of explicit public policy through the courts has moved people's practices into the realm of the assumptions underlying public budgeting and of private life, in which they can still live as they had before, yet minimize public support for those who are different and poor. As Carr explains, the segregated academies' "websites often display non-discrimination clauses—yet feature photos only of smiling white children."[10] They do not even tout "token" diversity, though tokenism is itself a prejudicial practice,[11] since they do not want diversity.

It is important to note some of the ways in which the disunity and injustice I have mentioned become manifest at other levels and in concrete experiences. First, given the traditional divisions I have highlighted, there has historically been racially different channeling of students. In particular, when African Americans graduated from high school with an interest in higher education, there were for a long time active efforts to steer them to community colleges only or to black colleges, now called Historically Black Colleges and Universities (HBCUs).[12] These schools certainly offer remarkable opportunities, yet when it comes to state funding, for instance, for the University of Mississippi's School of Pharmacy, the state has an interest in avoiding overlapping special university investments. At the same time, graduates from the School of Pharmacy can earn starting salaries in excess of $90,000 today. Therefore, when the University of Mississippi offered special programs and was segregated, it was tracking students into different levels of jobs, salary, and social capital from what other schools could offer. Today, with the explicit racial barriers to entry removed from colleges and universities,[13] the fact is that colleges still have requirements for standardized scores for admission, and also expectations of preparedness for students to succeed in college. The new barrier to entry on the road to open social mobility and opportunity today is the inadequacy of prima-

ry and secondary education for poor and minority populations. When the minimum score on the ACT for entry to
the University of Mississippi is sixteen,[14] and when that is
approximately the average score for African American students in the state (16.3), that means that a large number of
students fall below that level of preparedness, which is not
true of white students whose average score is over 20.6.[15] In
this sense, students are therefore tracked because of where
they grew up and because of their parents' poverty and lower levels of education.

Beyond these more general, yet tangible effects of the disunity and injustice embedded in Mississippian and American culture, there are at times outbursts of violence that
spring from the underlying vice of racism. I will end this
section with an example of terrible violence, but I hope that
readers will not think instances of injustice that lack physical
violence are somehow of small importance. I believe that the
following case of terrible hatred and violence is a development out of a culture of division and consequent injustice. It
demonstrates a cultural disrespect for the dignity and worth
of all people and the lack of any sense of the common good
across difference between citizens.

According to a 2013 FBI press release from the Justice
Department, Joseph Dominick, Deryl Paul Dedmon, John
Aaron Rice, Dylan Wade Butler, William Kirk Montgomery, and Jonathan Kyle Gaskamp, all aged nineteen through
twenty-three and all from Brandon, Mississippi, entered
guilty pleas in connection with their roles in a case of con-
spiracy to commit federal hate crimes. These crimes were in
connection with an assault on African Americans in Jackson, Mississippi.[16] The group's assault ended in the death of
James Craig Anderson, killed June 26, 2011. Anderson was a
forty-seven-year-old car plant worker whom the assailants

found outside of a motel. The young men beat Anderson, and then Dedmon got in his Ford F-250 and ran over Anderson, causing injuries that resulted in his death.[17] According to the Associated Press, "Police said Dedmon was driving the truck and later bragged that he ran over Anderson, using a racial slur to describe him."[18]

The Justice Department's press release issued in January 2013 explains further that

> on an occasion predating the death of Mr. Anderson, Dominick, Montgomery, Butler, and others known to the government traveled to Jackson in Dominick's truck for the purpose of finding and assaulting vulnerable African-Americans. . . . Dominick and his co-conspirators also purchased a sling shot and metal ball bearings to shoot at African-Americans and then took turns shooting the sling shot at multiple African-Americans they encountered.[19]

These young men had a history of racially motivated violence and also had discussed plans to assault African Americans the night before the attack, which was Dominick's birthday.

Early morning the next day, they committed acts which Daniel McMullen, special agent in charge of the FBI's Jackson field office, described as depriving "others of their civil rights based on the color of their skin, [and it] cannot be tolerated."[20] In addition, US Attorney John Dowdy argued that "the actions of these defendants who have pled guilty today in this court do not represent the values of Mississippi in 2012. This is an absolute tragedy, and what this family has had to go through as a result of the actions of these young men is inexcusable."[21] Having lived in Mississippi since 2007, I can certainly say that the hate crimes committed by these young men were shocking to me, yet they appear connected to the culture of hatred and division which plagues the state.

Democratic leadership with regard to justice in Mississippi cannot look only to the levels on the surface, where we see murders or low test scores. Appeals for change must draw on deep values underneath the surface, in the foundations of Mississippi culture, to find and make use of commonalities across difference. There are remarkable resources in the common Christian beliefs of the people here, yet Sunday mornings remain among the most segregated hour in America, as Martin Luther King Jr. was known to say.[22]

Beyond religious commonalities, there are some signs that more and more people are growing concerned about Mississippi's inadequate schools. Governor Winter, the state's "education governor," advanced education for all as a Democrat, with challenges often coming from those who prioritize keeping taxes low and thus limiting spending on education. Recently, however, Republican governor Phil Bryant has echoed Governor Winter's famous line. Governor Winter often instructed that "the only road out of poverty runs by the schoolhouse door." In January 2013, Governor Bryant delivered his State of the State Address, arguing that "it is imperative that we remember what others have also known—the path to Mississippi's economic success must pass through the schoolhouse door."[23] Bryant rightly shows us that an appreciation for the vital importance of education is a bipartisan concern.

Although at some very difficult moments I have despaired for the chances for change in Mississippi, I hold out hope for three reasons. The first is that fifty years ago, my African American students could not have enrolled at the University of Mississippi and become the remarkable successes that they have alongside or ahead of their peers. If that great a transformation can occur in fifty years, I believe in the potential of the next fifty years. The second reason is that some politicians set aside their wedge issues temporarily and sometimes do seek common ground, such as we may see after Governor Bryant's 2013 statements. Finally, the third and best reason is that I have known so many brilliant young people in Mississippi who participate in respectful experimental inquiry for the common good of the state and nation. They cannot abide the problems that Mississippians face, and they have the energy and talent to lead a meaningful movement for the sake of justice. For democratic leadership to change the fabric of injustice, division, and hatred, however, I have become convinced that what will be most profoundly needed are judicious yet courageous guides who focus on culture, values from top to bottom and from the bottom up. It is vital for leadership in Mississippi to recognize the deep-seated problems that plague the state. As I explained in the introduction to this book, I see value in adapting Faulkner's famous line, suggesting that to lead the world, you have to understand leadership for a place like Mississippi.

8.

POLICY NEEDS
AND INITIATIVES

My aim in this book has been to introduce some new ways of thinking, building on and updating classical ideas about the virtues of leadership. Necessarily, this task can only begin discussions that will require collaboration, focus, study, and experimentation. I have tried to incorporate some particular matters of policy and social practice, however, to offer some concreteness and to demonstrate the meaning of the theory of democratic leadership that I have presented. In this chapter, I will conclude with some brief summations of suggestions for initial policy priorities in Mississippi. These ideas are not presented with any intended order.

Communication. In his influential though technical book, *Experience and Nature* (1925), Dewey wrote that "of all affairs, communication is the most wonderful. . . . Where communication exists, things in acquiring meaning, thereby acquire representatives, surrogates, signs and implicates, which are infinitely more amenable to management, more permanent and more accommodating, than events in their first estate."[1] Dewey explained that communication is an activity which renders situations more manageable. It lays the foundation for addressing shared problems together in community. This is one of the reasons, for example, why it is important to talk more about taboo or difficult subjects, such as corporal punishment and sex education.

Many small towns in Mississippi do not have even a basic

newspaper or means of sharing communal information and dialogue. It is difficult for anyone to have a voice or community without channels through which to speak. The power of electronic communication and tools could be leveraged along with efforts to improve education and literacy. Communication ought to be established and advocated vigorously and tirelessly between the disparate communities of the state. It can also create channels through which citizens can easily find and contact their representatives. After all, if not only public officials but citizens as well bear responsibility for failures to make use of wisdom or to reflect the justified will of the people, channels of communication would be invaluable tools for greater leadership. Enhanced communication will empower citizens to participate together in public inquiry, the task of leadership that pursues democratic wisdom.

Churches will only reinforce the state's problems, furthermore, until they begin to welcome fellow community members of all kinds into their congregations—and invite others regularly, not only as guests, but as new members as well—which can begin and maintain communication between groups previously divided. Religious leaders have great power and responsibility and have for a long time failed to recognize them properly or use them substantially. It is worth emphasizing the place of communication in wisdom, in intelligent public inquiry, in achieving unity, and in highlighting commonality and shared concerns across difference. A campaign for building and activating channels of communication is a vital step in the pursuit of progress for Mississippi.

Address lowered educational standards, but only with added support. A common problem in poor parts of Mississippi concerns the difficulty of attracting, training, and keeping great teachers. Teachers who come to places like the Mississippi Delta are often shocked at how far behind their students are. Efforts to attract talent, including from our own state universities' graduating classes, and to enhance the teacher workforce must be among the state's top priorities. Governor Bryant's efforts to support Teach for America and Mississippi Teacher Corps are a start, but much more effort is needed. Among various reasons, one is that TFA teachers generally do not remain teachers beyond their commitment periods—one reason more permanent solutions are needed.

Great leadership must convince Mississippians that it is time to be courageous and to invest in the people and to attract an army of strong teachers to towns that are remote and poor. Consider, for example, that Como, Mississippi, said to have one of the worst elementary schools in America,[2] would offer a person with a college degree $33,390 per year according to the Mississippi Adequate Education Plan for the 2014–2015 school year.[3] North Panola County has been labelled a "critical shortage area" by the state Department of Education.[4] While the state's pay scale is graduated by education level, such that a person with a doctorate would earn over $38,000, these levels of pay are not filling critical shortages. The answer to what will work will take some experimentation. I suggest that pay levels be raised especially for critical shortage areas. If such targeted raises are somehow impossible, then, nevertheless, raised teacher salaries are a vital part of the solution. If teachers were offered salaries just $7,000 higher, say from $40,000 to $45,000, depending on their level of education, as a starting salary to work in Como, Mississippi, it is unquestionable that more teachers with higher qualifications would consider applying for such positions. Such a change would add up to a large number if applied to all of Mississippi's 32,000 teachers. However, the apparently large resulting difference in expenditure, roughly $224 million, would represent an increase of merely 1.25 percent of the state's $18 billion budget. This certainly does not add up all relevant costs, but it is important to see costs in relation to the state's overall budget. Big changes can be achieved with only one or two percent changes to the budget. It is worth noting that in March of 2015, the state legislature debated an income tax cut of $550 million over 15 years, despite clear existing needs in the state.[5]

Whenever one speaks in terms of millions of dollars, to you and me as individuals the numbers sound simply enormous. At the state level, however, a change of 1.25 percent can be achieved through a few steps together, such as small shifts in revenue sources like the income tax; property taxes; and so-called sin taxes; such as on alcohol and cigarettes— a less controversial form of sales tax. Increases in general sales taxes are reasonably resisted for being regressive— most negatively impacting the poor. A mixture of sources of funding like the three I have suggested, however, would mean a smaller change to each, diminishing impact on any one particular source of revenues. Another source of support could come from the funds that would come in if the presently debated tax cuts were shelved until education is sufficiently supported.

As a state with some of the lowest taxes in the country, we have considerable room before we even approach the middle of the bottom quintile of tax levels in the country. How these adjustments ought best to be made should go through serious debate and discussion. If a change is desperately needed, however, and it is, there is every reason to believe that it can be accomplished, given the will to try. The payoff of enhancing education in Mississippi, according to both Governor Winter and Governor Bryant, could well be the state's rise out of poverty. If that is correct, the choice to remain in poverty would represent failure of the state's citizens and officials to care sufficiently about all Mississippians and to have the courage to experiment and invest in educational growth for the sake of the overall well-being of the state. Of course, with decreased poverty, decreased incarceration, and greater earnings and business attraction due to a more educated workforce, some costs will decrease as a result while revenues also rise from increased incomes. It is time to set aside the dogged rhetoric resistant to public support for education and to make a change of one percent or more in the state budget. In 2014, as Mississippi's football teams have excelled, Governor Winter challenges us all, explaining that "I love how successful our football teams are! But if we can pay our football coaches $3 million, then we can certainly pay our teachers more!"[6]

Democratic values in education. Some think that we need religion in schools and say so because we need to teach students about ethics. Far less controversial is the call to teach ethics in schools without having to draw on any particular religious point of view. This latter approach is viable for public schools, in contrast with the former's conflict with the First Amendment of the US Constitution. Those who are strongly religious should not find this problematic if there are excellent ways to teach values that are shared and in common with Christian and other religious and nonreligious traditions or perspectives. A solution of this kind has been proposed and has yielded *New York Times* best sellers. I am referring to works by President Reagan's former secretary of education, William Bennett, who earned his PhD in philosophy. He wrote *The Book of Virtues: A Treasury of Great Moral Stories* (1996) for parents, and *The Children's Book of Virtues* (1995).[7] There is a rich tradition of teaching ethics by way of focusing on virtues, and it has its great American representatives, such as in Benjamin Franklin's eighteenth-century *Autobiography*, where he catalogued thirteen virtues and explained his efforts to live by them and to exercise his attention on embodying them in his behavior.[8]

A further element of rendering education more democratic is to prioritize reason-giving and respect for each person's worth and dignity in our schools. I have explained already why I believe that such democratic values require an end to corporal punishment in schools. What is needed in its place is the development of a welcoming and encouraging culture of celebration of success and participation in school. Trying to teach kids with violence is to act undemocratically, even if it is done for the sake of achieving democratic ends, what Dewey calls a great mistake. It also misses even Plato's lesson on the matter, namely, as I have argued, that you cannot teach people by force. In addition, attention to wisdom and intelligent public inquiry should drive decision making to policies that establish opportunities for comprehensive sex education for all students while offering an opt-out process for parents who wish for their children to be excluded from such curricular offerings.

Finally, we must not ignore the need and potential for educating adults, not only in our community colleges, but also in efforts to reach the parents of our younger students. Programs through which teachers involve parents (TIP programs) can be understood as educational programming for adults, but undertaken with existing resources. In addition, we have our community colleges, though persons living in poverty and who must work to make ends meet are often unable to return to school without supportive policies in place. Organizations like the Working Poor Family Project have proposed a number of particular policies that could maximize the potential benefits of adult education in Mississippi.[9] The benefits and need for education are not limited to the young.

Reversing the brain-drain. It is a common expectation that in Mississippi, many talented people will leave the state in search of greater opportunities. This is not inherently a bad thing. The same is true of Ohio and Georgia, though both states are considerably wealthier than Mississippi. The issue is that a great many talented people grow up in Mississippi but see few opportunities for themselves in the state. With some effort, public officials could create opportunities for young people to make a difference in Mississippi. In 2012, five of the University of Mississippi's top graduating students whom I worked with accepted positions with Teach for America and four of them decided to stay in the state to teach.[10] Still others have accepted opportunities for leadership and public action, such as through Mississippi Teacher Corps and other offices in state government. There are models in use around the country for offering incentives to young people to serve their state in exchange for help with expenses related to higher education. Mississippi could make use of such strategies as well. We have a teacher corps as well as federal programs like Teach for America and military service. I can imagine a Mississippi Development Corps, made up of young people who undertake efforts to enhance communication and address other needs as outlined here and around the state in a process of guided projects for community development.[11]

A culture of celebrated success. A minister and friend from Taylor, Mississippi, once told me that the problem in Taylor was that no one celebrates educational success.[12] What could be simpler than to hold events and opportunities for the recognition of educational successes? For one worry,

President Obama in 2008 criticized the celebration of students' completion of eighth grade. He said, "Now hold on a second—this is just eighth grade. So let's not go over the top. Let's not have a huge party. Let's just give them a handshake. . . . You're supposed to graduate from eighth grade."[13] The president's intention seems to be to make sure that people maintain the right priorities and celebrate especially the achievement of ultimate goals, not giving too much weight to partial successes. While there are differences about how and when celebrations should occur, we ought to celebrate success in education. The KIPP Delta schools certainly prioritize and celebrate the success of their seniors. On a visit to their schools, I was moved when I saw their main bulletin board featuring their seniors' letters of acceptance from colleges, highlighting great achievements that were plentiful, yet meaningful, and unusual and rare in the nearby traditional school. In short, policy initiatives can target educational culture, and more should do so. Just as a series of substantial efforts was organized to combat high school dropout rates,[14] we can also organize a series of researched, planned, and distributed resources for each school to use in enhancing cultural tools and practices for celebrating educational achievement.

Spending on education. I have alluded to the need to invest in Mississippi's future. There is little doubt that people are right when they say you cannot throw money at a problem and think it will simply be fixed. That does not mean, however, that additional spending is unimportant or unnecessary. When in a car, confronted with a curb or a steep hill, small amounts of added gas may only end in frustration with no success at traveling to one's destination. Nevertheless, it is often the case that giving the car considerably more gas will indeed get you moving. If our military security were at risk, no price in dollars would seem too high to address the problem. It is time we recognize that education in Mississippi is in a state of profound crisis deserving of the support necessary to address our public challenges.

There is no value in ignoring or sugarcoating what must be done. The state must spend considerably more money on education, and do so wisely. I have mentioned a figure in relation to teacher salaries. Teacher shortages and the need for more qualified teachers are two central challenges for Mississippi, but not the only ones. At the same time, there are those who think that government expenditures are always inefficient, yet even they would rarely raise such concerns about the spending that they deem to be essential, such as with military spending. In addition, I have been truly amazed by my experience at the University of Mississippi, a state-run educational institution, which inspires more pride among alumni and citizens than I have ever seen directed to a university. To put matters into perspective, the institution's annual operating budget for 2012–2013 was $1.94 billion. So if one were to speculate about differences that could be made in terms of millions of dollars, such a sum to address schools all over the state is only a small fraction of the funds expended on one of our state's major universities. State institutions can be run effectively, such as our state's public universities, and can merit the respect and admiration of the people.

When it comes to wise investment in the efforts of education, the key here concerns the attraction of scores of talented educational administrators and teachers and bringing them to remote and poor regions of the state. To remember the scope of the problem, consider that Iowa, with a population size that is similar to Mississippi's and with a highly rural distribution of its citizens, was said to have seven "dropout factories," according to a 2007 Associated Press report, compared with Mississippi's forty-four.[15] So long as people wish to spend as little as possible on public education, this crucial democratic imperative will go unfulfilled, as will Mississippi's potential. Among the appendixes, I have included a piece I published in the *Clarion Ledger*, titled "Teachers Offer Hope."[16] There, I argued that when things are going poorly in life and in many circumstances, fixing one's problems costs considerably more than funding operations that are already going smoothly. By the same token, then, it should be expected to cost *more*, considerably more, to fund properly efforts to turn failing schools around, let alone ones that are remote and in tougher circumstances to attract strong teachers. Until Mississippians are spending as much or more on schools than many other states, we are not considering the challenge of attracting quality teachers to towns like Como, Mississippi, or to offering a quality education and an excellent set of life opportunities to our young people irrespective of their backgrounds. It is simply very difficult to attract quality teachers to remote and poor areas, and therefore more effort, in the form of money, opportunity, and recognition, will be necessary to bring about great change. If I am right in seeing moral growth as having great potential to yield economic growth, my argument in chapter 1, then investments in our people will pay great dividends.

CONCLUSION

Much more could be said about how to address the problems I have outlined in this book. It is vital, however, to recognize the variety and depth of Mississippi's challenges. We can gain insight from the key virtues of the good society, and therefore of good leadership. It is unacceptable for a democratic society to tolerate the systematic classification of some people as inferior or less important, which the state's education system implies. The directives I have presented in broad strokes here are initial considerations for ways to begin an attack on the vices that plague the state. They are also proposals promising great progress. Mississippi is a state whose stock is undervalued. Investing in ourselves and our people has great potential for growth. Leadership is not only about fixing existing problems, but also a matter of envisioning realizable possibilities for excellence in the future. I can imagine remarkable development in Mississippi's economy, population, and visibility in the nation and in the world. If Atlanta, Georgia, was able to bring the Olympics to town in 1996, Mississippi could consider other, perhaps at first smaller efforts, building toward the kind of attractions that lead eyes, and therefore minds, to consider living, working, and employing great people in Mississippi.

When I once asked students here whether Mississippi could attract the Olympics, they laughed—not that such an event is itself needed or particularly suited to the goals I have noted in this book. To skeptics, however, I offer the University of Mississippi as an example. The university hosted the first 2008 presidential debate after nearly two decades of energy and resources were invested in numerous successful efforts to develop the university. I have been told on many occasions that people twenty years earlier never could have imagined that the University of Mississippi would host a presidential debate.

Bright visions for the future of Mississippi depend on the great strides still to be made in race relations, education, and poverty alleviation. Good democratic leadership must aim to guide the state's culture toward respect for the dignity and worth of all citizens. It demands the courage to experiment and to try out sincere efforts for change. It calls for taking advantage of well-established wisdom and for understanding leadership as a process of shared inquiry itself. Finally, democratic leadership must aim for the common good of all, and in manners that are themselves democratic and unifying. These four virtues are the key elements of democratic leadership, I believe, and have much to offer for moral and political progress in Mississippi, the United States, and other democratic societies.

ACKNOWLEDGMENTS

I am grateful to many people for helping me to make this project a reality. I received the strongest support from my first department chair at the University of Mississippi, Robert Haws. Haws believed in engaged scholarship that reaches beyond academia. He was eager to see his fellow faculty members practice such engaged work. He also was a knowledgeable colleague with a deep understanding of Mississippi and of American history, and his input was generous and valuable. I value his counsel still today when I have the fortune of speaking with him since his retirement.

More recently, two colleagues read early drafts of this project and encouraged me to present the ideas developed here to general audiences, especially in Mississippi and in the South. Susan Glisson, director of the William Winter Institute for Racial Reconciliation, and Jody Holland, a colleague in the department of Public Policy Leadership, both offered me feedback and reason to believe that the ideas presented in this book are needed in Mississippi. In addition, Susan introduced me to Governor Winter, who also reviewed this work and offered me invaluable encouragement and feedback. I am exceptionally grateful to Governor Winter for his generosity and support in writing the Foreword for this book. We need more statesmen and courageous leaders like him.

Before I met Susan or Jody, I learned about Governor Winter and the potential for progress in Mississippi from Andy Mullins, who when I met him was serving as chief of staff to the University of Mississippi chancellor Robert Khayat. Mullins's book, *Building Consensus: A History of the Passage of the Mississippi Education Reform Act of 1982* (1992), demonstrated the potential for change even in the face of strong resistance and division.

A number of courageous students inspired me as I developed on this book. In particular, I owe thanks to Brian Barnes, Brent Caldwell, Melissa Cole, Andre' Cotten, Christopher Cox, Melody Frierson, Caleb Herod, Nick Luckett, Jake McGraw, Taylor McGraw, Hope Merrell, Brannon Miller, Cortez Moss, Hunter Nicholson, Abby Olivier, Artair Rogers, Mary Alex Street, Lexi Thoman, and Rachel Willis.

At different stages in the development of this project, I benefited from feedback from colleagues Kenneth Townsend, David Rutherford, Melissa Bass, and Mark Van Boening. I also benefited enormously from comments and encouragement I received from Elizabeth Anderson, the John Rawls Professor of Philosophy at the University of Michigan. In numerous ways my former graduate school colleague Tommy Curry, now associate professor of philosophy at Texas A&M University, offered me invaluable feedback and suggestions for further reading on topics concerning democracy, politics, and race.

I have been immeasurably fortunate to have the continuing support of three people who have been sources of great inspiration. Many people are lucky to have one mentor. I have been blessed with two. John Lachs, Centennial Professor of Philosophy at Vanderbilt University, and Larry Hickman, director of the Center for Dewey Studies at Southern Illinois University, have offered me wise guidance time and again. My wife, Annie Davis Weber, is one of my toughest critics and editors, yet also my best and most patient friend. She inspires me every day.

Next, I am grateful to photographer Bruce Newman and to Lexington Books. Newman granted me permission to use his photograph of the "We Are One Mississippi Candlelight Walk" (2012) for the cover. Lexington Books published my longer and more theoretical book titled *Democracy and Leadership: On Pragmatism and Virtue*, released in 2013, from which the present book is an extension. Lexington Books also generously granted me permission to reuse, deepen, and update material that was first published in *Democracy and Leadership*. Readers who would like a fuller account of my theory of democratic leadership should look to that earlier work.

I am grateful also for generous support from interim Dean Richard Forgette of the College of Liberal Arts and Provost Morris Stocks at the University of Mississippi. Both supported my research on this project over the years, including some of the time I was able to dedicate to it over the course of my 2014 sabbatical period. Finally, I appreciate the encouragement I have received at numerous times in the last few years from University of Mississippi chancellor Dan Jones, who kindly visited my Philospohy of Leadership class in the spring of 2015.

APPENDIXES

Included here are seven op-ed articles that I published with the intention of contributing to inquiry into democratic values in Mississippi. I offer these as examples of advocacy for issues I believe to be important for good democratic leadership. I include them also as demonstrations of the value that philosophical ideas can bring to bear on real-life problems. These pieces were published in the *Clarion Ledger*, *Science Progress*, and *ProBizMS .com*. In each piece, I was representing only my own point of view. I am grateful to the *Clarion Ledger* (http://www.clarionled ger.com/), to *Science Progress* (http://scienceprogress.org/), and to *ProBizMS.com* for their permission to republish these articles. The articles included here are the following:

1. "Choosing Civility: The Lemonade Lesson."
2. "Cultural Divides: Barriers Remain to Educational Attainment."
3. "Greening Industry and Green Industries in Mississippi."
4. "Mississippians Are Ready for Comprehensive Sex Education."
5. "Teachers Offer Hope for Mississippi."
6. "Try Charters Schools Experiment Where Others Failing."
7. "Violence Taught When Corporal Punishment Used."

APPENDIX 1

Choosing Civility: The Lemonade Lesson

Originally published in the *Clarion Ledger* on September 19, 2010, 8B-9B, included with permission.

On a hot summer day, young girls gave out lemonade in their neighborhood. The fact that they were not charging for their kindness launched columnist Terry Savage of the *Chicago Sun-Times* into a rage. According to Savage, these girls were the problem with America and a symptom of it.

Savage yelled "No!" at the girls and berated them. They were giving away their parents' property, Savage thought, assuming that the girls had no allowance of their own to use as they pleased. She failed to imagine that their parents intended to instill a spirit of giving in their children. To her the only point of a lemonade stand is to learn about business, never about the value of charity or kindness. Just think of how mad Savage must be about Jesus's miracle of feeding the multitudes, which according to her logic, contributed to inflation and involved giving away his father's property.

The lemonade story is a clear example of the problem of incivility in America. In his recent book, *Democracy and Moral Conflict*, philosopher Robert Talisse has argued that incivility is one of the greatest threats to democracy in our country. National Endowment for the Humanities chairman Jim Leach, a thirty-year Republican congressman from Iowa, has been touring the country to talk about the great need for civility today. Talisse and

Leach have noticed the rise of incivility in the country and are as concerned as I am about it.

Incivility has been severe many times in the last few years. In 2007, MoveOn.org took out a large advertisement attacking US General David Petraeus. Sounding like mean-spirited school children, they asked: "General Petraeus or General Betray Us?"

More recently, town hall meetings around the country devolved quickly into screaming matches in which detractors wanted to avoid sincere debate about the need for health care reform. US Rep. Joe Wilson's outburst during President Obama's 2009 speech before Congress was equally troubling, though he has since apologized. Often the same people criticize President Obama for spending too much and then admonish all efforts to find cost saving strategies for reforming health care. Our problems are too big to be solved with partisan attacks and the avoidance of debate.

Conservative David Frum was right on target when he argued that unwillingness to engage in civil debate on health care reform meant that Republicans missed a real opportunity to shape the legislation that passed. Shortly after Frum made these remarks, he was dismissed from the American Enterprise Institute, though his following has since grown.

At a time when oil and tar balls have devastated the coastal environment and economy in Mississippi and nearby states, we need civility profoundly. With high unemployment and low funds for Medicaid, we need political cooperation. Americans must tone down the virulence that plagues our debates. The disasters we face offer an opportunity to return to civility, to bring people together to address common problems.

It is fair to ask what civility is, after all. It sometimes sounds like what old people prefer or what the privileged classes call for when oppressed people rise up. No, civility is not necessarily a pacifist ethic. It is a set of at least three moral tenets.

The first rule of civility calls for open and intelligent public debate by means of respectful communication. This rule is broken when people falsify information or inflame the public against understanding groups who disagree. For instance, when Michael Moore shows only the devastation of job losses in Michigan in his film, *Roger and Me* (1989), he omits any consideration of what happens when American companies fail to remain competitive. The disturbances of the town hall meetings on healthcare are another example of violating this rule.

The second tenet of civility demands respect for fellow citizens—that we see them as stakeholders and sources of insight about what keeps democracy afloat. One way to break this second rule is to demonize opposition. For example, the North Iowa Tea Party put up a billboard that, according to AP, "showed photographs of President Obama, Nazi leader Hitler and communist leader Lenin beneath the labels 'Democrat Socialism,' 'National Socialism,' and 'Marxist Socialism.'" Fortunately, the Tea Party members in Iowa came to see that the sign reflected poorly on them and they removed it.

It is difficult to imagine civil discourse between people who demonize each other. Consider CNN's reports in 2009 that "threats on the life of the president of the United States have now risen by as much as 400 percent since [Obama's] inauguration . . . [which] 'in this environment' go far beyond anything the Secret Service has seen with any other president." This year, past anger about the president's Christian pastor has been replaced with the contradicting pretension that he is a Muslim. Not only are these developments and the conflict over the building of mosques in New York and Tennessee disturbing for their efforts to demonize opposition, but they also treat Muslims as though they don't deserve the same freedom of religion as the rest of us. As citizens and voters, we must demand that our leaders address our real problems as a nation instead of stoking prejudices.

Fortunately, we have a chance to make such a statement this November.

The third rule of civility calls for respect for public institutions. In the heat of the moment, it can be difficult to accept the slow bureaucratic processes of the courts, but public institutions do something very important when they slow us down. They force us to wait, to allow anger to cool, and to let reason take over. Time and calmness are needed for intelligent thought and discussion. Without them, we get vigilantism, as in the murder of Dr. George Tiller in Kansas.

Of course, respect for public institutions does not mean that we must avoid criticizing them. In fact, in America, criticism is a chief virtue. It is the most powerful tool for reforming unjust, ineffective, and wasteful practices. In that sense, then, respect for institutions requires scrutiny and criticism. These things are only meaningful, however, if it is possible for institutions to do better than they do. So, even civil criticism of public institutions implies optimism about the promise of better democratic governance.

Civility is not an empty term. It represents a class of virtues that we must foster in schools and in public debates. If constitutional democracy is worthwhile, it is because of its potential for intelligent social action. It can help the greatest number of people to be happy while respecting the rights of those who would fight even against civility itself.

We must not follow Savage's example. A civil answer to an offer of lemonade is "thank you." America today needs voices to be civil. The battle for civility is endless, to be sure, but without it we debase democracy and choose moral blindness over vision.

Appendix 2

Cultural Divides:
Barriers Remain to Educational Attainment

Originally published in the *Clarion Ledger*, June 6, 2010, 1C-2C,
included here with permission.

Mississippi appears to be stuck in a vicious Catch-22, which accompanies the state's troubled racial history. On the one hand, Gov. Haley Barbour has noted that education is the No. 1 economic development issue in the state. At the same time, poverty and racial stereotyping inhibit educational success. The problem appears irresolvable.

Two reactions are common. The first one says things are not so bad in Mississippi—the denial of failure. The second sees failure everywhere and expects nothing else of the state—the prophecy of failure. Exceptional students who overcome adversity are proof for the deniers and negative stories about Mississippi are confirmation for the prophets of failure.

Both views are troubling. Most people have a hard time denying the state's great problems. Some think that if only we would quit pointing out Mississippi's troubles, we could get people to invest here and to grow business. There is some truth to this concern, but ignoring real problems only lets them grow. My own optimism for the future of the state comes from the fact that the Catch-22 is only apparent. It can be overcome. The difficult problem falls on the side of the pessimists. They create and sustain self-fulfilling prophecies of failure.

A self-fulfilling prophecy is an error of reasoning. When

people commit this fallacy, they call some circumstance inevitable and then, through their own actions or inaction, they make it true. The conclusion they draw from the experience is that they were right: the outcome was inevitable.

Take an example from baseball. A kid who says he will never get a hit decides not to swing. When the third strike whizzes by, he says "See! There was no way I was going to get a hit!"

Failure in baseball has miniscule effects compared with failure in school. Imagine the same thought process at work when a student believes that he or she cannot succeed on a test. If messages continue to predict poor students' failure in education, we should not be surprised when some think there is no point to school.

A number of my students told me about their experiences in transition to college and gave me permission to pass on their messages. The first four are African-American students and the fifth is white. Christopher Cox said: "My high school guidance counselors told me that coming from my background that I would struggle during my tenure. They said that I should attend junior college. This increased my doubt in myself being able to achieve at a four-year institution . . . these statements were discouraging," he said.

Chris will be a senior in the fall at the University of Mississippi and has a bright future ahead of him.

Nick Luckett shared with me the fact that some members of his community warned him against coming to UM in particular. They told him "Don't go there. You'll get killed." This warning was likely to have been racially motivated.

But other teachers told him he would be better off attending a community college, rather than a four-year institution, advice with economic implications. He explained: "Despite all the negativity I received because I decided to come to Ole Miss, I have had a great experience here at this university and I am so glad that I came."

Next, Andre' Cotten and Melissa Cole, both inductees in the UM Student Hall of Fame, have related difficult transitions to college. Andre' wrote that "from my experience, I find that some prospective minority students get discouraged because of the stigma of social injustice that some people who are not familiar with the Ole Miss community attach to our university . . . on the contrary, from my experience as an undergraduate I found that there seems to be a comfortable place for everyone to fit within the Ole Miss family."

Melissa explained that "when I told my friends, neighbors and fellow church members that I would attend Ole Miss, I was always asked 'Why?' or was received with a frown." Certainly racial history played an important role in the culture that inspired these forms of discouragement, but it is important to notice the economic impact that comes along with it.

Finally, Brent Caldwell, one of my white students,[1] has explained to me that he has "a few friends whose parents didn't go (to college) and who gave them the attitude of 'well we didn't need to go to school; why do you?' . . . Unfortunately, most of these friends never went on to college or flamed out of community colleges." Brent explained that between himself and his former friends, he experienced a "palpable feeling of class difference there," which ended a number of his friendships.

In examples like these I see a symptom of what appears to be happening at all levels in the state. There is still an outlook that inspires people to think that certain institutions and successes are not "for us," for poor African Americans or whites, or for Mississippians generally. These attitudes are observable at many levels, despite the shining examples that contradict them.

The cultural challenges for Mississippi impact us all. When people get too used to hearing negative things about Mississippi, they become more likely to accept low expectations for the state.

We need the opposite. We need high expectations, but without denying the problems we face.

Something very important for cultural leadership is at work in the examples of the successful students I have mentioned. I have asked my students how they overcame discouragements from going to college or from coming to the University of Mississippi.

Their answers are often that "I knew her" or "I knew him." Students saw examples of success and wanted it for themselves. A crucial component of leadership in educational attainment in Mississippi must come from a few individuals who swim against the powerful currents of discouragement. When they succeed, others can see that their own prospects might also be bright. The more our students succeed and are visible, the harder it becomes to assume that failure in school is the only option.

My proposal to overcome the apparent Catch-22 is simple: We must fight culture with culture and on many fronts. One way I suggest we do it is with a documentary. There are countless examples of success that we can show kids in Mississippi to contradict the harsh discouragements that many children confront. We have rich resources in our fantastic students who must be talked about, who must be shown to others as the exemplars that they are. A growing number of students have overcome self-fulfilling prophecies of failure. With a documentary we can highlight our many successful students.

We can make the video available for classrooms and public television, but we can also post it online for each student to watch through our expanding avenues of communication that technology has enabled. I envision a viral video that students can access directly on computers at school or in local libraries, to circumvent the common channels of discouragement.

Such efforts could be just the kind of force needed to turn today's cultural current around, to replace a negative and discouraging culture with a culture of excellence.

Appendix 3

Greening Industry and Green Industries
in Mississippi

Originally published on *ProBizMS.com*, April 8, 2012, included here with permission. This article is available at https://www.academia.edu/3000337/.

For quite some time, people have associated environmentally focused efforts with the Democratic Party, and hence with partisan disagreements. Fortunately today people are coming to see that environmental friendliness generally saves money and is a cause motivating big business development. Mississippi could benefit from greater understanding of environmentally friendly developments. There are many opportunities for industry to save money through greening efforts and also for businesses to expand in the areas that service demand for green technologies and energy saving investments.

President Carter put up solar panels on the Whitehouse [*sic*], which were soon after removed in Reagan's administration. Then, Vice President Al Gore came to be well known for his advocacy on environmental issues, to the point that he has been a key spokesman for related movements. Opposition to environmentally beneficial technologies was often motivated by a desire to keep industry free from excess government imposition. Plus, religious motivations were at times raised, with the explanation that the Earth was created for mankind's use. Human beings have dominion over the Earth, so why not make use of it as we please?

In the last few years, a number of factors have refocused discussions about the environment. First, rising gas prices have called into question for many the wisdom of driving Hummers, for instance. I suspect that they might be incredibly fun to drive in obstacle courses, but regular travel would be hugely expensive in one, compared with the great, fuel efficient cars that are taking over the market. In a Toyota Prius, for example, my family and I can drive to Atlanta, 6 hours away from Oxford, MS, on slightly less than 10 gallons of gas. With regular driving in the last few years, the fuel efficient car has been fantastic for us. Whether one feels for environmental considerations or not, people can understand the savings.

It helps, I think, to note the differences between people's experiences of environmental forces. For example, having lived near New York City, then in Atlanta and Nashville, I saw recycling efforts everywhere I have lived. There are prices associated with landfills. The farther away are the landfills, the more fuel is spent bringing trash to dumps. Plus, the slower one fills a dump, the cheaper it is—the more delayed further costs are. So, recycling in my experience has always had a clear and substantial impact economically on large population centers I have known. Now that I live in Mississippi, by contrast, land is quite cheap and the motivation for recycling is far weaker here. Add that to the history of associating the practice with the minority political party in the state and it becomes easier to understand why the recycling movement has only lately caught on in small towns in the state.

Two developments, one at the national level and the other at the state level, have inspired some changes as well. Historically strong critics of people like Al Gore, such as Rupert Murdoch, who owns News Corp and thus Fox News and the Wall Street Journal, have come to see the powerful forces of environmental change. Murdoch saw the spreading wildfires in his native Australia and understood quickly that climates have changed, leading to dangerous conditions for a number of parts of the world. He wrote a letter called "Duty to the Future," published on the *National Review Online*, explaining why his companies were going green. Beyond Murdoch, Pat Robertson has helped reshape the religious message on the Right about the environment, to recognize the idea that dominion over the Earth is consistent with the demands of stewardship of such a great gift from the Divine. He made a fun commercial with Reverend Al Sharpton for the sake of seeking common ground about the environment.

The second development is that Mississippians recently experienced significant environmental problems. People all around were saddened by the photos of wildlife affected by the B.P. oil spill. Mississippi's shrimping and coastal tourism industries were deeply affected for some time. Beyond that, many people who have been quiet about the environment, but who have loved it all along have begun speaking up. In particular, I am thinking of hunters, who love the outdoors, the beauty of creatures and the connection to the world that capturing your own food can motivate. In fact, people often forget that the environmental philosopher Aldo Leopold was a hunter.

A bright conservative student of mine at the University of Mississippi, Elliott Warren, had a number of these connections click. His love of hunting and the outdoors motivated action and leadership for green initiatives on campus. He was so driven and successful that he won a Sustainability Leadership Award the next year at the University of Mississippi. He is centrally responsible for the great program of game-day recycling for football games at the university, which has kept literally tons of waste from going into the ground. Instead, the new program provides the city of Oxford with materials that it can sell to companies seeking cost-saving recyclables.

With all of these developments in the background, there are nevertheless those who are skeptical of "green" initiatives, like the one the University of Mississippi signed a few years ago. However particular people feel about this initiative, there are great examples of substantial savings already at work on campus, and ones that can be emulated in various ways by businesses around the state.

I work in Odom Hall, which is one of the wings of the building called the Trent Lott Leadership Institute. I have learned from campus sources that our building in peak hours uses 65 to 70 Kilowatts per hour for its power. Nearby, the newly built Center for Manufacturing Excellence, a larger building, had solar panels installed on its roof. The panels do not provide all the power for that building, to be sure, since it is a very large building. But, they do provide more in peak hours than my building uses in its peak hours. Those panels produce 80 to 90 Kilowatts per hour in their peak hours. They generate 8 megawatts per month on average, according to Professor James Vaughn, Director of the Center for Manufacturing Excellence at the university.

Investments in technologies like the panels atop the Center for Manufacturing Excellence may not yet be feasible for widespread use in homes or in smaller businesses around the state, of course. But, technologies like these are getting cheaper and cheaper to make. Plus, there are countless efforts that are low in cost to adopt. A student of mine years ago gave a speech in one of my courses and convinced me to change to compact fluorescent bulbs around the house. The next month, I saw a drop in my electricity bill from the previous month and in comparison with the year before. The initial investment was about $150 for all new bulbs. Many people are using low water usage toilets and shower heads now, for similar reasons. Better insulation can make a big difference in the summer heat as well, of course, and all of these efforts are small and accessible ways that business can shave costs.

Those larger institutions that have to do maintenance with some regularity, furthermore, such as the university, which has projects and updates to complete each year, can budget for the long-term benefits of doing things in the smartest way with regard to energy. Many of these ideas involve small changes, but can make a difference to the bottom line. Plus, when one makes an effort in this way, we can brag about it to those who will be attracted by the idea. My favorite Oxford dry cleaner, Rainbow Cleaners, for example, posts notices about the new methods it uses to cut down on waste products and energy use. Plus, companies that profit from doing what is less responsible, morally speaking, sometimes get hit hard in lawsuits, when the results really hurt people, or in public image at least, which is itself a very expensive thing to clean up once tarnished.

Beyond the process of making industry "greener," there is also exciting growth taking place in Mississippi in "green" industries. Both of these terms, "greening" industry and "green" industries, are worth encouraging. "Greening industry" is the process of making industries and institutions more energy efficient, which makes for savings in money and from unwanted environmental effects. It can include cutting costs on public schools and other government buildings as well as in introducing cost saving measures in the private sector. Next, "green industries" are generally associated with things like electric windmills, fuel efficient cars, and solar panels, but they refer equally, in my view, to the sale of products and services that somehow take advantage of more energy efficient means of production or usage, or of products made from materials that cost less environmentally speaking.

Green products can be quite simple, not always technical in nature. When shopping at Walmart, if you have not tried out their great reusable bags, you have no idea what you are missing. They cost 50 cents each. I use these bags every day for all sorts of reasons, including for carrying my lunch to work or groceries home from the store. Granted, you have to pay for these once, but they are much more comfortable to carry than everyday plastic bags—given their thick handles—and they hold much more and more robustly, all while being light to carry. Plus, they are strong, have many uses, and also are made of reusable plastic that would otherwise eventually cost us money to throw in landfills.

The more sophisticated forms of "green industries" are growing also, and in Mississippi. Among these are Twin Creeks, Stion, and Soladigm, to name a few. A former student of mine landed a job right after graduation in 2011 with one of these companies and had only exciting things to report about his experience.

There are other countries and other states fighting to be at the forefront of business development in green industries. There are also other states doing more with tax incentives than we do in Mississippi to empower individuals and institutions to green their workplaces. At the same time, Mississippi has advantages for attracting business and can build on these, including low taxes. We can also work to take advantage of the recent developments through which people have come to see that "green" is not a partisan issue. It is at times a matter of cost savings and at others of potential new markets. We should welcome our new opportunities and think about how we can build on them for cost savings and profit. Here at the University of Mississippi, where tuition is around $6,000 per year, we can envision energy savings translating into the language of scholarships made possible per month, for example. When buildings cost thousands of dollars per month to power, the value of alternate energy sources that can offset big institutional costs becomes easier to imagine and understand.

If you are thinking of moving in the direction of energy cost savings only, there are do-it-yourself options available at places like Home Depot, which has a great guide online about all manner of products that can save money and energy in the long run. There are many more of these as public awareness continues to grow.

We can all see that gas prices at best will only rise more slowly even if new sources are found. It makes a lot of sense for business people to think of long-term investments. We can save money, and make more too, by thinking about industries that until recently seemed only to be of interest to small numbers of Mississippians. Today, minds have changed and a culture has set in that recognizes the need and opportunity for growth in green industries and in greening industry.

APPENDIX 4

Mississippians Are Ready for Comprehensive Sex Education: Social Science and Public Opinion Polls Agree

Originally published in *Science Progress*, February 14, 2012, included here with permission from *Science Progress* (http://www.scienceprogress.org). This article can be found online at http://scienceprogress.org/2012/02/mississip pians-are-ready-for-comprehensive-sex-education/.

Mississippi will surprise you. A recent Gallup poll found it to be the "most conservative state," yet Mississippi's voters rejected the personhood initiative in late 2011. But another development about reproductive health in Mississippi has gone largely unnoticed and deserves a closer look.

In December 2011 the Center for Mississippi Health Policy released a report titled "What Do Mississippi Parents Think about Sex-Related Education in Public Schools?" I expected to see a strong reluctance to have comprehensive sex education in public schools. The common political ideology suggests that educating children about sex is a parent's responsibility, not that of the government.

The related inclination is to think that demonstrating condom use will only teach students that having sex before marriage is acceptable. Such judgments ignore the facts. A 20-year study published in the January 2007 issue of *Public Health Reports* shows that premarital sex has been the norm since at least 1940. The study published in 2007 shows that of thousands of subjects surveyed, 95 percent of respondents between the ages of 15 and

44 had engaged in premarital sex. Plus, 75 percent of respondents had done so by the age of 20. These developments are not recent. The study showed in fact that "the number of Americans having premarital sex hasn't changed much since the 1940s," as Jennifer Warner put it for WebMD.

The 2011 Mississippi survey on sex education showed surprising results. Mississippi parents are overwhelmingly in favor of age-appropriate, comprehensive sex education. Marie Barnard, who is a parent of public school kids in Oxford, Mississippi, and the assistant dean of applied sciences at the University of Mississippi, believes that "it is a minority of parents" who oppose comprehensive sex education in the public schools, but "they are very passionate about their beliefs and are active in influencing their local school boards." So it seems that despite the great popularity of comprehensive sex education, a vocal minority is in control.

Sex education is an important topic in Mississippi. We have some of the highest rates of teen pregnancy and poverty, aggravated by some of the lowest rates of educational attainment in the country. Each of these factors can spur the others. A young woman in a school with inadequate sex education is more likely to become pregnant than one with comprehensive sex education. If she becomes pregnant, she is much more likely not to complete school. Having a child, furthermore, will limit her ability to work full time, diminishing the already low income she will earn if she does not complete high school.

The common refrain we hear from politicians in Mississippi is that there is only one sure way not to become pregnant, which is to abstain from having sex. Beyond the fact that 75 percent of Americans have sex before the age of 20, the crucial fact is that scholars have offered conclusive evidence showing that comprehensive sex education is "the most effective approach to reducing STDs and pregnancy." This statement was the conclusion of a 2010 Rutgers study published in the *Archives of Pediatrics and Adolescent Medicine.*

At the same time it is worth noting that abstinence-only sex education is effective for some limited groups. According to a Rutgers news release about the 2010 study, an "abstinence-only program helped sixth and seventh graders delay high-risk sexual behaviors up to two years after the initial intervention." But "nearly a quarter of these sixth and seventh graders had already had sex by the time they became a part of [the] study." The study highlighted an underappreciated lesson: "Sex education is not about teaching one topic to one age group and that's it. It has to start at the earliest ages, build upon and reinforce the previous knowledge and skills learned, and evolve as students get older and become more likely to start having sex."

In Mississippi the state passed House Bill 999 in 2011, which requires that all schools in Mississippi adopt a sex education policy by the end of June 2012. Mississippi First, a nonpartisan nonprofit advocating for effective, data-driven policy in the state, strongly urges "comprehensive or 'abstinence-plus' education—because it works," following the established lessons learned in countless studies.

Unfortunately, the Mississippi law allows school districts to choose between abstinence-only and abstinence-plus sex educa-tion. So some school districts will choose a more comprehen-sive form of sex education from which objecting families could opt out of the lessons beyond abstinence for their children. But others will teach abstinence-only education, offering no op-tions for those who want comprehensive programs. Even those abstinence-plus districts, however, "shall not include instruction and demonstrations on the application and use of condoms," ac-cording to the law. Advocates for comprehensive sex education such as the Sexuality Information and Education Council of the United States argue that "there are many youth who still need to learn how to prevent errors in [condom] use." Nevertheless, the Mississippi law against such instruction is clear.

Barnard heard a parent opposed to comprehensive sex education claim that "his disagreement with abstinence-plus was based on his religious beliefs." She responded that "Our children deserve a comprehensive, factually accurate, nonjudgmental education that is not based on a few individuals' personal religious beliefs, but on scientifically validated educational programs." The comprehensive approach with an opt-out mechanism would respect both views, but some districts will not choose it.

One might expect Mississippians to be generally opposed to comprehensive sex education, given the legislation that passed, but Barnard is right. The December 2011 study from the Mississippi Health Policy Center undercuts the common misconception.

First, 92 percent of the 3,600 parents responding were in favor of some form of sex education, which refers either to abstinence-only or abstinence-plus education. Abstinence-only would exclude, among other things, education about the use of contraceptives. The surprising result of the study, however, was that 89.8 percent of survey respondents said that they either "strongly support" (78.4 percent) or "somewhat support" (11.4 percent) education about birth control methods. The total opposition to the teaching of birth control methods came from fewer than 8 percent of respondents.

Despite the overwhelming support for education about birth control, some Mississippi students will be stuck with their school district's decision to teach abstinence-only sex education. This is a serious problem. The approach taken has been to deny some kids education, rather than to offer it with an opt-out policy approach.

Even the most controversial element of sex education in Mississippi, particularly the classroom demonstration of proper condom use, was in fact supported by a large majority of Mississippians. While 15.2 percent of respondents "strongly oppose" and 7.1 percent "somewhat oppose" classroom demonstrations of condom usage, 53.9 percent "strongly support" it and 17.2 percent "somewhat support" it. That means overall that 71.1 percent of respondents support in-class condom demonstrations, which the state's sex education law wholly forbids for all schools.

The Center for Mississippi Health Policy's December 2011 study shows that Mississippians are misunderstood and poorly represented. It is now up to school districts to choose the more effective approach to sex education—abstinence-plus forms instead of abstinence-only curricula. Perhaps in the next few years the legislature will have the courage to require that all schools provide comprehensive sex education—including condom use—while offering parents the choice to opt out of portions for their own children as they see fit.

Appendix 5

Teachers Offer Hope for Mississippi

Originally published in the *Clarion Ledger*, April 8, 2012, 1C-2C, included here with permission.

Former Gov. Haley Barbour once called education Mississippi's No. 1 economic development issue. Former Gov. Winter often said that "The road out of poverty runs by the schoolhouse."

Two recent developments are reasons to be hopeful about education in Mississippi. For one, a number of extraordinary graduating college students in Mississippi have made it into Teach for America and the Mississippi Teacher Corps, both very selective programs.

The second story is that Governor Phil Bryant and Lieutenant Governor Tate Reeves call for budget increases for TFA and MTC, requesting increases of $12 million and $1 million, respectively. The programs address the need for more teachers in the state. Thus, increased support would make a difference.

These developments are good news, even if criticisms are raised when leaders depend too much on such programs. To appreciate both points of view, we can say that TFA and the MTC do great work, but they do represent temporary solutions to our long-term educational challenges. Overall, the best news is that many of our brightest students are looking to serve the state and the country in this vital area.

TFA and MTC are special programs that bring some of the brightest new college graduates to teach in impoverished areas. Both programs are attracting truly remarkable talent.

In 2011, TFA received 48,000 applications from around the country, according to Regional Communications Director Kaitlin Gastrock. Only 14 percent of applicants were accepted. MTC, a state program, received 380 applications last year and accepted only 10 percent of those. As a reference, TFA's acceptance rate is more selective than what you find in undergraduate admissions to Vanderbilt, Duke, and the University of Chicago.

TFA and MTC are drawing a great deal of interest and are selecting from very strong applicants. This year, a number of University of Mississippi students were accepted into these competitive programs. Both categories include a number of Honors College students and one is a Phi Beta Kappa honoree. These are some of the strongest students at the University of Mississippi.

MTC Program Manager Ben Guest has argued that teacher quality and availability are two of the most important areas of need for Mississippi's schools. He thinks that the state should significantly increase teacher salaries to draw strong career teachers.

At the same time, he advocates for MTC and TFA as temporary measures, until the public will is garnered to undertake bigger, needed investment.

Guest and others think that TFA throws underprepared teachers into some of the most challenging classrooms in the country. Professor Deborah Appleman of Carleton College argued in 2009 that teaching takes a great deal of preparation, and TFA provides only a very brief introduction to the practice.

On the issue of preparation, studies are inconclusive. Some, such as the 2004 Mathematica Policy Research study, are favorable about the outcomes from TFA-taught students.

Other studies, such as Linda Darling-Hammond's 2005 study, show some results of TFA classrooms to be below average. Variations will always occur in teaching, of course, and more study is needed.

Nevertheless, Guest and Appleman argue for more robust

teacher preparation processes, given long-term goals for public schools. Measures like MTC and TFA are valuable in the short-run, furthermore, but could be used as excuses not to make larger investments in increased teacher preparation and salaries to fill the need for career teachers.

The standard reply to calls for increased salaries is that "more funding is not the solution." Two points are worth considering here.

The first is that unless we are spending considerably more than other states with higher rates of educational attainment, the assumption is untested. According to a 2009 US Census Bureau report, Mississippi spent $8,919 per pupil per year. By contrast, Pennsylvania, Maine, and Alaska each spent more than $15,000 per pupil while yielding stronger graduation rates than Mississippi's, according to the New America Foundation.

The second point is that troubled and failing schools can require more money per pupil than successful schools, and beyond any present differences in funding. Bigger challenges normally come with higher price tags.

Modest increases in funding may not make much difference, as the key challenge suggests, but substantial investments very well could. My favorite analogy is that hopping a curb in a car may not work with only small nudges on the gas. More substantial efforts, however, more gas, might get the desired result.

Guest recognizes that big changes are difficult to achieve, of course. He and others do what they can to address deep problems in our schools with programs like TFA and MTC, but not without recognition of the programs' limited goals and reach.

There is more value to both the teachers in TFA and MTC and their students than people commonly recognize. First, there are few settings as rich for professional development as classrooms. The classroom is one of the most extensive systems where the rubber meets the road every day in terms of public policy's connection to real-life challenges. Plus, in the mechanics of the classroom, teachers learn about people and communities that they were unfamiliar with before.

They gain public speaking skills, facilitation skills, as well as political acumen as they navigate personalities and hierarchies within the schools.

A further benefit gained from TFA and MTC teachers goes beyond class material, in exposing kids to talented and caring young college graduates. Cultural obstacles often impede progress in addressing both poverty and educational attainment. For if students are unable to imagine themselves successful in school, why try? TFA and MTC participants can help their students to imagine themselves as young college graduates.

Participants in TFA and MTC may go on teaching or may run for local or state office after their service. They certainly have substance to draw on for making policy recommendations about education in Mississippi once they finish. Given the professional development that occurs in the classroom, prospective employers should be eager to hire alums of TFA and MTC. Consider what effect two years of maturation beyond college yield for those who go through the programs.

Participants have demonstrated their interest in service and have refined their abilities as communicators, critical thinkers, and leaders. These programs benefit participants in ways that will last throughout their careers.

Even with these virtues, TFA and MTC are not panaceas. They offer a path for talented students to serve their state or country. The programs keep talented people in the state and draw talent from elsewhere. Praise for the programs should not discount the important considerations that Appleman and Guest raise, however: that TFA and MTC are not substitutes for adequately funded schools and competitive teacher salaries.

Nevertheless, we have reason to celebrate. A large group of

brilliant college graduates are looking to serve the state and the nation. Plus, the calls for support from the governor and lieutenant governor inspire hope that increased support for education and the will to pursue lasting progress are growing.

Appendix 6

Try Charter Schools Experiment Where Others Failing

Originally published in the *Clarion Ledger*, March 6, 2010, 9A, included here with permission.

In January, three University of Mississippi undergraduates advocated for charter schools before the Mississippi House Committee on Education out of concern for the crisis of education in the state. The Public Policy Leadership majors, Chelsea Caveny, Cortez Moss, and Alex McLelland, met resistance to partial measures for progress.

Aside from a few vocal opponents, the general response from Republicans in the room was positive and some Democrats were cautiously open to charter schools. The most vocal opponents of charter school legislation worried about the children who stay behind in traditional schools. One representative exclaimed: "Separate but unequal!"

I can understand the resistance. If charter schools only help some, are they not institutions that tell others to wait? Dr. Martin Luther King Jr. had to explain time and time again "why we can't wait." He was a great opponent of the numbing gradualism of his day. Being patient is not something suffering people can easily stomach. Despite this powerful motivation, however, the objection to gradualism is misapplied when it comes to charter schools. Charter schools represent the potential, certainly not a guarantee, for substantial progress in education in the state.

At the committee meeting in January, three worries arose. First, if charter schools are the answer, why not overhaul the whole system to follow their method? In response to this concern, the issue is not a desire for progress to be slow. Rather, what is needed is sincere experimentation. In different states and regions, different methods work well or poorly. Charter schools need fine-tuning. Good experimenters, furthermore, don't stop after one try. Once a model is successful in our state, we should replicate it then and then only, as the urban prep schools did in Chicago.

The second worry that our legislators raised was that charter schools may not work as well in rural areas. There are clear exceptions to this concern, however, such as the KIPP schools (Knowledge Is Power Programs) which have locations in Helena-West Helena, Ark. What seemed to be lacking in the legislators' responses to the students' presentation was the will to try, to experiment with new ideas. Innovation and change require openness of mind to the possibilities that others may not have attempted.

A final concern came up. In the accusing charge of "separate but unequal!" was the reasonable worry people have about achievement gaps between white and minority students. This week, the House version of the charter school legislation made sure to emphasize that charters could be established only in replacing schools with a three-year track record of failure. This requirement would ensure that charters be created only where schools most need help, not simply as alternatives for already advantaged students.

Charter school legislation is moving forward for consideration. What is crucial for the future of Mississippi, I believe, is that we regain the will to experiment and to try new ideas. Charter school legislation may only be a partial measure, a step in a larger plan.

With good legislation written to allay the worries people have about charters, however, the charter school initiative could represent a great step forward and in the right direction.

APPENDIX 7

Violence Taught When Corporal Punishment Used

Originally published in the *Clarion Ledger*, May 14, 2013, 9A, included with permission.

The harsh treatment of prisoners in the United States causes much controversy, yet in our public schools, institutionalized violence is commonplace.

In April, the *Hattiesburg American* reported that corporal punishment declined in Mississippi schools between 2007 and 2012 from more than 58,000 reported instances to around 39,000.

The use of corporal punishment varies greatly by school district. For the Lafayette County School District's roughly 2,700 students, there were seven recorded cases of corporal punishment in the 2009–2010 school year and none the following year. By contrast, the Quitman County School District enrolls just under 1,300 students, yet recorded 1,594 instances of corporal punishment in the 2010–2011 academic year, which is only about 180 school days.

In the United States, all 50 states permit corporal punishment in domestic settings. For public and private schools, however, only 19 states still practice it, while in Iowa and New Jersey it is illegal to perform in schools.

Iowa is a helpful state to use in comparison with Mississippi, since it is largely rural and has a comparable population size. Of course, Iowa has its problems, with seven schools districts named "dropout factories" in a 2007 Associated Press report. The same report called 44 of Mississippi's schools "dropout factories."

At best, corporal punishment in schools is not helping Mississippi. At worst, it is part of the problem.

According to studies, most parents find spankings in the home to be acceptable. It is important to distinguish parenting from schooling, however, and to watch out for institutional excesses. The 1980 federal case *Hall v. Tawney* said that excess corporal punishment in schools could violate a student's "right to ultimate bodily security, the most fundamental aspect of personal privacy, (which) is unmistakably established in our constitutional decisions as an attribute of the ordered liberty that is the concern of substantive due process."

Not all spankings in schools might be called excessive, of course, yet cases reported on in the *Hattiesburg American* raise serious concern. In 2011, 14-year-old Trey Clayton of Independence High School was paddled so severely that he fainted, "fell face-first onto the concrete floor . . . (and) had five shattered teeth and a lacerated chin," according to reporter Marquita Brown.

Beyond legal concerns and the tragically severe cases, there are strong reasons to end institutionalized corporal punishment.

First, students are compelled to be in school, and with good reason. Democratic societies must educate citizens to be self-governing. Yet Plato and other philosophers believed correctly, I think, that learning cannot take hold by compulsion. Socrates argued that "nothing taught by force stays in the soul."

Compulsory schooling can address Plato's worry, however, by showing students the value of education. It is vital to create an environment in which education is welcoming and inviting. Corporal punishment has the reverse effect.

Second, corporal punishment teaches students that when confronted with a challenge, adults use violence rather than reason to achieve our ends. It solidifies "school-to-prison pipelines" that the Justice Department is combating.

In Mississippi, we know that culture matters and that many of our schools are struggling. Corporal punishment is only one element of a culture which discourages students. Ending the practice, however, would contribute meaningfully to the reconstruction of an encouraging and positive culture of achievement in education.

NOTES

Epigraph

1. This statement is often attributed to William Faulkner, but to my knowledge is not found in his published works. Howry professor of Faulkner Studies Dr. Jay Watson of the University of Mississippi has told me that he is unaware of the origin of the quote, yet says that it is ubiquitous in writings about Faulkner. For one of many secondary sources where the quote is found without statement of its published source, see Eugene R. Dattel, "Cotton in a Global Economy: Mississippi (1800–1860)," *Mississippi History Now*, http://mshistorynow.mdah.state.ms.us/articles/161/cotton-in-a-global-economy-mississippi-1800-1860.

Introduction

1. Patti Hassler, "Families Struggle: Child Poverty Remains High," *Children's Defense Fund*, September 20, 2012, http://www.childrensdefense.org/newsroom/cdf-in-the-news/press-releases/2012/child-poverty-remains-high.html (accessed January 25, 2013).

2. The Annie E. Casey Foundation, "Kids Count Data Book: State Trends in Child Well-Being, 2012," http://www.kidscount.org.

3. These numbers come from the Kids Count online database, http://www.datacenter.kidscount.org/data/bystate/.

4. This particular detail comes from an Associated Press source, which has catalogued "Dropout Factories." See Johns

Hopkins Researchers, "Dropout Factories: Take a Closer Look at Failing Schools across the Country," *Associated Press*, 2007, http://hosted.ap.org/specials/interactives/wdc/dropout/. If one counts as a graduation rate the proportion of seniors who graduate, the graduation rate will appear far higher than if one counts the number of eighth graders who complete their senior year of high school.

5. The remainder of these details, not counting the one reference in the previous note, are drawn once again from the Kids Count database.

6. Sid Salter, "Charter Schools Offer Alternative to Mediocre/Failing Schools," *Desoto Times Tribune*, February 22, 2012, http://www.desototimes.com/articles/2012/02/23/opinion/editorials/doc4f453f741ac69454084633.txt (accessed January 23, 2013).

7. This was Rawls's insight in his presentation of the "difference principle," the idea that inequalities are acceptable only so long as they are reasonably believed to be of benefit for all. For instance, if all people have a morally acceptable set of living conditions, for some who are successful or fortunate in business to earn considerably more money than others can in many circumstances be of benefit to all, insofar as all gain from the products he or she sells. See John Rawls, *A Theory of Justice* (Cambridge, MA: Harvard University Press, 1999), 65. Plato was deeply concerned about great differences of wealth and poverty, especially when those differences foster disunity and disharmony in a society. Were Rawls to reply directly to Plato, I believe that he would suggest that it is possible for differences of wealth to exist in such a manner that each person benefits, such as when a medical scientist gets wealthy creating a medicine that makes everyone healthier and happier. He would agree, however, that it is also possible for differences of wealth to render people's lives worse off, and that, he claimed, was the limiting factor between just and unjust social structures that produce great differences of wealth and poverty.

Those social structures that permit the improvement of life conditions for the best off at the expense of the least advantaged citizens in society are unjust, on his view.

8. Here I have in mind John Dewey, "Attacks Wage Disparity," in *The Collected Works of John Dewey, The Later Works*, vol. 5, *1929–1930*, ed. Jo Ann Boydston (Carbondale: Southern Illinois University Press, 1988), 431. First published in the *New York Times*, December 26, 1929, 28.

9. My understanding is confirmed in Oliver Thomas, "A Poverty, Not Education, Crisis in U.S.A." *USA Today*, December 11, 2013, 8A.

10. As I mentioned in the note for the Epigraph, above, this quote is ubiquitous in the literature on Faulkner yet does not occur in his published works. Still, it is accepted as one of his sayings.

11. Benjamin Friedman, *The Moral Consequences of Economic Growth* (New York: Vintage Books, 2005).

12. Students of mine who have visited South Africa have drawn for me a number of comparisons between Mississippi and that country. Their histories both featured great inequalities and injustices on racial grounds. The persons of black African descent in both places are deeply impoverished. Finally, a profound need exists in both places for racial and moral reconciliation. While I mention South Africa here in this passage, my focus centers on Mississippi. Nevertheless, I believe it useful to note that Mississippi is not alone in raising some of the concerns that I am referring to here.

13. The Honorable William Winter. See Mississippi Center for Education Innovation, "About Us: Planting Seeds . . . Charting Courses," Learning Labs, 2008, http://www.kellogglearninglabs.org/upload_main/docs/ms-aagd-web_09-03-19.pdf (accessed January 26, 2013).

14. Larry A. Hickman, gen. ed., *The Correspondence of John*

Dewey, 1859–1952, 2nd edition, ed. Barbara Levine, Anne Sharpe, and Harriet Furst Simon (Charlottesville, VA : InteLex Corp., 2001), 1891.06.03 (00460). I am referring to a letter that Dewey wrote to William James in 1891. I discuss this letter and related themes in an essay, Eric Thomas Weber, "James, Dewey, and Democracy," *William James Studies* 4 (2009): 90–110, esp. 95–100.

Chapter 1

1. As a brief start, see Mississippi Economic Council, "Executive Summary of Momentum Mississippi's Economic Development Incentive Legislation Proposal," http://www.msmec.com/mx/hm.asp?id=execsumbp. See also Marianne T. Hill, *Mississippi Economic Review and Outlook*, 22, no. 1 (2008). Finally, see The Special Task Force for the Revitalization of the Delta Region, ed., *Mississippi Delta Revitalization: Goals and Recommendations 2008* (Jackson, MS: Mississippi Delta Strategic Compact, 2008), http://www.mississippi.edu/drtf/downloads/delta_task_force_recc_for_2008.pdf.

2. Tami Luhby, "Mississippi Has Highest Poverty and Lowest Income," *CNN Money*, September 20, 2012, http://money.cnn.com/2012/09/20/news/economy/income-states-poverty/index.html. Last accessed 1/26/13.

3. See Richard Vedder and Bryan O'Keefe, "Wal-Mart against the Wall?," *Washington Times*, August 27, 2006. Vedder and O'Keefe defend Walmart against a number of Democrats.

4. Robert Nozick, "Why Do Intellectuals Oppose Capitalism? (Excerpted)." *Cato Policy Report* 20, no. 1 (January–February 1998), http://www.libertarianism.org/publications/essays/why-do-intellectuals-oppose-capitalism.

5. Friedman, *The Moral Consequences of Economic Growth*, 4.

6. Ibid., ix.

7. See Nicholas D. Kristof and Sheryl WuDunn, "The Women's

Crusade," *New York Times Magazine*, August 23, 2009, MM28, http://www.nytimes.com/2009/08/23/magazine/23Women-t .html. One might object by pointing out that the standard of living for women in such countries is rising, even if slowly. It seems clear to me, however, that recent changes have been brought about by a constellation of factors, not the least of which was the Arab Spring, in which many Arab nations began to question the injustice of tyrannical rule. Donna Abu-nasr, "Saudi Women Get in the Driver's Seat; Flout Licence Ban," *National Post* (Toronto), June 18, 2011, A23.

8. N. Gregory Mankiw, David Romer, and David N. Weil, "A Contribution to the Empirics of Economic Growth," *Quarterly Journal of Economics* 107, no. 2 (1992): 413.

9. For a few examples, see Thorvaldur Gylfason and Gylfi Zoega, "Natural Resources and Economic Growth: The Role of Investment," *World Economy* 29, no. 8 (2006): 1091–1115; Kevin B. Grier and Gordun Tullock, "An Empirical Analysis of Cross-National Economic Growth, 1951–1980," *Journal of Monetary Economics* 24 (1989): 259–76; Mohammed Omran and Ali Bolbol, "Foreign Direct Investment, Financial Development, and Economic Growth: Evidence from the Arab Countries," *Review of Middle East Economics and Finance* 1, no. 3 (2003): 231–49; Yousif Khalifa Al-Yousif, "Exports and Economic Growth: Some Empirical Evidence from the Arab Gulf Countries," *Applied Economics* 29, no. 6 (1997): 693–697; and Khalifa H. Ghali, "Government Spending and Economic Growth in Saudi Arabia," *Journal of Economic Development* 22, no. 2 (1997): 165–72.

10. Gwenn Okruhlik, "Networks of Dissent: Islamism and Reform in Saudi Arabia," *Current History* 101, no. 651 (2002): 22–28.

11. The best example of this process is in health care. Because advantaged citizens have insurance, the price that can be paid by many for treatment is much higher. The market price rises accordingly, making it harder for uninsured people to afford care.

I made this point in greater detail in an op-ed in the *Clarion Ledger* (Jackson, MS) in 2011. See Eric Thomas Weber, "Liberty, Health Care Reform Fit," *Clarion Ledger*, January 30, 2011, 13B.

12. See Johannes G. Hoogeveen and Berk Özler, "Not Separate, Not Equal: Poverty and Inequality in Post-Apartheid South Africa," *William Davidson Institute Working Paper*, 739 (January 2005): 1–41.

13. John Rawls, *Political Liberalism* (New York: Columbia University Press, 1996), xviii–xx.

14. Terry Frieden, "Mississippi Town Sued over 'School-to-Prison Pipeline,'" *CNN*, October, 26, 2012, http://www.cnn .com/2012/10/24/justice/mississippi-civil-rights-lawsuit/.

15. Andrew Peterson, "Mississippi Manufacturing: Toyota Completing Mississippi Plant for Corolla," *Motor Trend*, June 17, 2010, http://wot.motortrend.com/mississippi-manufacturing-toyota-completing-mississippi-plant-for-corolla-8985.html.

16. Alan Reynolds, "Lower Tax Rates Mean Faster Economic Growth," *Creators.com*, November 14, 2002, republished on the Cato Institute's website, http://www.cato.org/publications/com mentary/lower-tax-rates-mean-faster-economic-growth (accessed January 26, 2013).

17. Cornel West, *Democracy Matters: Winning the Fight against Imperialism* (New York: Penguin Books, 2005), 4.

18. In a report by the Economic Policy Institute, Robert Lynch writes that "too often public officeholders first embrace lowering taxes and creating tax incentives as their chief economic development tools, with public investment usually ranking as a distant third option. An analysis of the relevant research literature, however, finds little grounds to support tax cuts and incentives—especially when they occur at the expense of public investment—as the best means to expand employment and spur growth." Robert G. Lynch, *Rethinking Growth Strategies: How State and Local Taxes and Services Affect Economic Development* (Washing-

ton, DC: Economic Policy Institute, 2004), http://epi.3cdn.net/
f82246f98a3e3421fd_04m6iiklp.pdf, vii.

19. Bloomberg Bureau of National Affairs (BNA), "Most and
Least Taxing States 2012," *Bloomberg.com*, April 13, 2012, http://
www.bloomberg.com/money-gallery/2011-09-14/most-least-
taxing-states.html (accessed January 26, 2013).

20. Ibid. One might ask about Texas as an example of a
wealthy state with low taxes. My claim was not that no states can
be wealthy with low taxes, but rather that low taxes are not sufficient for delivering economic growth. Many factors make Texas
unique.

21. Harold Meyerson, "An Ongoing Civil War," *Washington
Post*, April 13, 2011, A15. To be sure, Meyerson adds that this
"Southern underinvestment" is threatening to become the "national norm." Florida has aimed to attract industry by keeping
taxes quite low but has come under criticism in the past decade.
Meyerson argued that "the state's economic progress will be
held back unless Floridians are willing to spend more on education." See Helen Huntley, "For Floridians, the Tax Burden Is Even
Lighter," *St. Petersburg Times* (Florida), April 9, 2004, 1A.

22. According to the US Census Bureau, in 2003 Mississippi's
poverty rate was 18.3 percent, compared with 12.5 percent for the
country. In 2008, the state had a poverty rate of 21.9 percent, and
in 2012 it rose to 22.6 percent. Therefore, while it is good news
that a number of manufacturing companies are "booming" in
Mississippi, overall trends for the state are moving in the opposite direction—toward more poverty, not less. See Micheline
Maynard, "With GE, Toyota, Nissan, Manufacturing Booms in
Mississippi," *Forbes*, July 10, 2012, 44–46, http://www.forbes
.com/sites/michelinemaynard/2012/07/10/with-ge-toyota-nissan
-manufacturing-booms-in-mississippi/.

23. Some of the strong advocates of minimalist government
will point to examples of businesses that have moved or started

up in Mississippi, such as the few car manufacturing plants or energy-related companies. When I use the term "largely" here, my point is to suggest that the state needs vastly greater development than it is achieving at present to pull its citizens out of deep poverty. See the previous note for the data concerning the recent increase in poverty, despite the opening of some car manufacturing plants.

Chapter 2

1. John Dewey, "Attacks Wage Disparity," in *The Collected Works of John Dewey, The Later Works,* vol. 5, *1929–1930,* ed. Jo Ann Boydston (Carbondale: Southern Illinois University Press, 1988), 431. First published in the *New York Times,* December 26, 1929, 28. I include here in the text the date of this piece, since it helps to contextualize his reference to a moral maxim that is pronounced often during the Christmas holiday season.

2. Paul Kurtz and John Shook, eds., *Dewey's Enduring Impact: Essays on America's Philosopher* (Amherst, NY: Prometheus Books, 2010).

3. Robert B. Westbrook, *John Dewey and American Democracy* (Ithaca, NY: Cornell University Press, 1991), ix.

4. Ibid., 542.

5. John Dewey, *Democracy and Education* (New York: The Free Press, 1944). Also published as John Dewey, *Democracy and Education,* in *The Collected Works of John Dewey, The Middle Works,* vol. 9, *1916,* ed. Jo Ann Boydston (Carbondale: Southern Illinois University Press, 1980). The title "Patron Saint of Schools" came from Henry T. Edmonson III, *John Dewey and the Decline of American Education: How the Patron Saint of Schools Has Corrupted Teaching and Learning* (Wilmington, DE: Intercollegiate Studies Institute, 2006).

6. Editors, "The Two Points of View on Education," *New York Times*, March 18, 1923, 3.

7. I. L. Kandel, "The Influence of Dewey Abroad," *Teachers College Record* 31, no. 3 (1929): 239–44; Gert J. J. Biesta and Siebren Miedema, "Dewey in Europe: A Case Study on the International Dimensions of the Turn-of-the-Century Educational Reform," *American Journal of Education* 105, no. 1 (1996): 1–26; A. Harry Passow, "John Dewey's Influence on Education around the World," *Teachers College Record* 83, no. 3 (1982): 401–18.

8. See Erika Lenkert, *Frommer's Memorable Walks in San Francisco*, 6th ed. (Hoboken, NJ: Wiley, 2006), 70.

9. Edmonson wants to separate Dewey from association with Jefferson, yet the effort is odd. Edmonson III, *John Dewey and the Decline of American Education*, 61. Dewey believed himself to be profoundly influenced by Jefferson's thinking on the need for the public to be educated. Westbrook, *John Dewey and American Democracy*, 454–55. Edmonson thinks that a big part of the problem of American education is the bureaucracy of federal direction, but to associate Dewey with such problems is to go looking for a symbol to scapegoat. As Jay Martin has explained, "John Dewey admired Thomas Jefferson above all other Americans." Jay Martin, *The Education of John Dewey* (New York: Columbia University Press, 2002), 14.

10. Letter from Thomas Jefferson to Uriah Forrest, December 31, 1787, in *The Papers of Thomas Jefferson*, vol. 12, ed. Julian P. Boyd (Princeton, NJ: Princeton University Press, 1955), 478. I am grateful to Rachel Willis for pointing out to me this passage from Jefferson.

11. Ari Helo and Peter Onuf, "Jefferson, Morality, and the Problem of Slavery," *William and Mary Quarterly* 60, no. 3 (July 2003): 583–614.

12. Sarah Carr, "In Southern Towns, 'Segregation Academies' Are Still Going Strong," *The Atlantic*, December 13, 2012, http://

www.theatlantic.com/national/archive/2012/12/in-southern
-towns-segregation-academies-are-still-going-strong/266207/
(accessed July 30, 2013).

13. John Dewey, "Ethical Principles Underlying Education," in *The Collected Works of John Dewey, The Early Works,* vol. 5, ed. Jo Ann Boydston (Carbondale: Southern Illinois University Press, 2008), 54–83, 59.

14. For recent and vehement religious criticism of Dewey's impact on education, though poorly tied to Dewey's actual contribution, see Edmonson, *John Dewey and the Decline of American Education.*

15. See "Understanding High School Graduation Rates in Mississippi," *Alliance for Excellent Education,* July 2009, http://www.all4ed.org/files/Mississippi_wc.pdf.

16. If we ask how many seniors graduate high school, the proportion will be far larger than when we ask how many juniors, sophomores, freshmen, or eighth graders eventually complete high school, each resulting successively in lower proportions. The Alliance for Excellent Education issued a report in 2009 highlighting the fact that Mississippi's "state reported [graduation rate] for NCLB" was 87 percent, while the US Department of Education's assessment assessed the state's graduation rate at 64 percent and *Education Week*'s evaluation called the rate 61 percent. See "Understanding High School Graduation Rates in Mississippi," 2009, and Johns Hopkins Researchers, "Dropout Factories."

17. For the 2008–2009 school year, a "dropout prevention plan" was drafted and implemented. Since that time, Canton's graduation rate rose to 62 percent in 2011. See Dwight J. Luckett, "Roadmap to Success: Dropout Prevention Plan, 2008–2009," Canton Public School District, 2008, http://www.mde.k12.ms.us/docs/dropout-prevention-and-compulsory-school-attendance-library/canton-public-school-district.PDF, and Mississippi

Center for Public Policy, "MS High School Graduation Rates, 2010–2011," *MCPP Reports*, http://www.mspolicy.org/mcpp_re ports/mcpp_reports_view.php?entryID=334. The MCPP's report was informed by the Mississippi Department of Education's data released for the 2010–2011 school year.

18. Mississippi Center for Public Policy, "MS High School Graduation Rates, 2010–2011."

19. I am thinking of Edmonson's *John Dewey and the Decline of American Education*.

20. Nate Jones, "Want to Be Class President in Mississippi? You Need to be White," *Time*, August 27, 2010, http://newsfeed .time.com/2010/08/27/want-to-be-class-president-in-mississip pi-you-need-to-be-white/.

21. Ibid.

22. Ibid.

23. David Germain, "Morgan Freeman Pays for Integrated Prom in New Documentary," *Huffington Post*, January 16, 2009, http://www.huffingtonpost.com/2009/01/16/morgan-freeman -pays-for-i_n_158628.html.

24. Associated Press, "More Mississippi Students Unprepared to Start College," *WTVA, NBC News Affiliate*, June 3, 2012, http:// www.wtva.com/news/local/story/More-Mississippi-students -unprepared-to-start/tbHxrmht9oe9fnaTGRP61g.cspx. Last accessed 1/26/13. See also Ben Wolfgang, "Scores Show Students Aren't Ready for College," *Washington Times*, August 17, 2011, A1, http://www.washingtontimes.com/news/2011/aug/17/scores -show-students-not-ready-college/. Wolfgang calls attention to Mississippi's results in the area of ACT scores, which are tests of preparedness for college. As I have said and as Wolfgang notes, Mississippi's results fall in last place.

25. This fact is especially visible in the Associated Press's chart for Mississippi in its "Dropout Factories" resource, http://hosted .ap.org/specials/interactives/wdc/dropout/. See Kenneth T. An-

drews, "Movement-Countermovement Dynamics and the Emergence of New Institutions: The Case of 'White Flight' Schools in Mississippi," *Social Forces* 80, no. 3 (2002): 911–36. On the effects of these kinds of segregation, see Gary Orfield, "Schools More Separate: Consequences of a Decade of Resegregation," in *Harvard Civil Rights Project* (Cambridge, MA: Harvard University, 2001): 1–55, http://www.eric.ed.gov/PDFS/ED459217.pdf.

26. Associated Press, "Dropout Factories."

27. Frieden, "Mississippi Town Sued."

28. Sam Dillon, "States' Data Obscure How Few Finish High School," *New York Times*, March 20, 2008, A1.

29. Peter Whoriskey, "By the Mississippi Delta, a Whole School Left Behind," *Washington Post*, October 28, 2007, A03.

30. Ibid.

31. US Census Bureau, "Profile of General Population and Housing Characteristics: 2010," *2010 Demographic Profile Data*, 2011, http://factfinder2.census.gov/faces/tableservices/jsf/pages/productview.xhtml?src=bkmk.

32. Maureen Downey, "Feds Release New High School Grad Data Using Common Yard Stick," *Atlanta Journal-Constitution*, for the *AJC Get Schooled Blog*, November 26, 2012, http://blogs.ajc.com/get-schooled-blog/2012/11/26/.

33. In fairness to Mississippi, results since 2007 have improved. See R. L. Nave, "Graduation Rates, Test Scores Up," *Jackson Free Press*, August 29, 2012, http://www.jacksonfreepress.com/news/2012/aug/29/graduation-rates-test-score/.

34. ACT, Inc., "2012 ACT National and State Scores," *The ACT*, 2012, http://www.act.org/newsroom/data/2012/states.html.

35. Kim Severson, "Mississippi Tells Public Schools to Develop Policies Allowing Prayers," *New York Times*, March 16, 2013, A13.

36. Gang Guo, "The Timing of the Influences of Cumulative Poverty on Children's Cognitive Ability and Achievement," *Social Forces* 77, no. 1 (1998): 257–87.

37. Doris Nhan, "Analysis: How Much States Spend on Their Kids Really Does Matter," *National Journal*, October 23, 2012, http://.nationaljournal.com/thenextamerica/education/analysis-how-much-states-spend-on-their-kids-really-does-matter - 20121016 (accessed January 26, 2013).

38. Ibid.; Kids Count database, datacenter.kidscount.org/. I should qualify that this dollar amount combines state and federal support.

39. Nhan, "Analysis."

40. See Eric Thomas Weber, "Cultural Divides: Barriers Remain to Educational Attainment," *Clarion Ledger*, June 6, 2010, C1–2. As I have said, it is also included here as Appendix 2.

41. Eric F. Dubow and Maria F. Ippolito, "Effects of Poverty and Quality of the Home Environment on Changes in the Academic and Behavioral Adjustment of Elementary School-Age Children," *Journal of Clinical Child Psychology* 23, no. 4 (1994).

42. Ibid., 401–402.

43. I originally learned that "deltas" generally refer to the place where rivers meet the sea. The "Mississippi Delta," by contrast, refers to a place where the Mississippi River often flooded, on its way to the sea, leaving sediment and rich nutrients behind that rendered the soil exceptionally rich and fertile. That area is in fact in the northwestern part of the state, not the portion of the river in the southern area where it reaches the coast.

44. KIPP Delta Public Schools, "Benchmark Exam: Results from Spring 2012," 2012, http://www.kippdelta.org.

45. To be sure, there are debates about the effects of school uniforms. On the one hand, uniforms lend a formality and seriousness to school endeavors. On the other, they can appear to limit freedom and raise costs for education, among other concerns. See Daphne Meadmore and Colin Symes, "Keeping Up Appearances: Uniform Policy for School Diversity?," *British Journal of Educational Studies* 45, no. 2 (1997): 174–86, and

Daphne Meadmore and Colin Symes, "Of Uniform Appearance: A Symbol of School Discipline and Governmentality," *Discourse* 17, no. 2 (1996): 209–25.

46. Brittany Watkins, "Rural, Poor, Successful: Every Arkansas KIPP Delta Grad Accepted into College," *Clarion Ledger*, February 16, 2013, http://www.clarionledger.com/article/20130217/OPINION03/302170002/.

47. Eli Hager, "Still Separate and Unequal," *Washington Post*, May 14, 2012, A13.

48. Ibid.

49. Scott Shirley, "For Students, 'Zip Code Does Not Define Destiny,'" *Take Part*, November 28, 2012, http://www.takepart.com/article/2012/11/28/kipp-delta-zip-code-not-define-destiny.

50. Whoriskey, "By the Mississippi Delta."

51. Andrew P. Mullins, *Building Consensus: A History of the Passage of the Mississippi Education Reform Act of 1982* (Waynesboro, MS: The Phil Hardin Foundation and the Mississippi Humanities Council, 1992), esp. chap. 1, "The Education Governor."

52. Shelly Sigo, "Mississippi: Gov. Oks $3.5b for Schools," *Bond Buyer*, May 2, 2007.

53. See my piece, Eric Thomas Weber, "Teachers Offer Hope: Teach for America Teacher Corps Draw Top Students but Aren't Panaceas," *Clarion Ledger*, April 8, 2012, C1–2. This piece, included in the Appendix, cites critics Ben Guest and Deborah Appleman.

Chapter 3

1. Eric Thomas Weber, *Democracy and Leadership: On Pragmatism and Virtue* (Lanham, MD: Lexington Books, 2013).

2. Malcolm Moore, "Thousands Line Street to Mourn Policeman Killed in Football Riot," *Daily Telegraph* (London), February 6, 2007, 15.

3. Mollie Reilly, "Chris McDaniel Accuses GOP of 'Abandoning the Conservative Movement' after Runoff Loss," *Huffington Post*, June 25, 2014, http://www.huffingtonpost.com/2014/06/25/chris-mcdaniel-republicans_n_5528041.html.

4. Norman J. Ornstein, "Reagan Was a Master of the Art of Compromise," *New York Times*, November 13, 2012, http://www.nytimes.com/roomfordebate/2012/06/11/could-ronald-reagan-lead-todays-gop/reagan-was-a-master-of-the-art-of-compromise.

5. Alastair Jamieson, "Scotland Rejects Independence in Record-Breaking Referendum," *NBC News*, September 18, 2014, http://www.nbcnews.com/storyline/scotland-independence-vote/scotland-rejects-independence-record-breaking-referendum-n206876.

6. See the Marketplace Fairness Act Web site, http://www.marketplacefairness.org/support/ (accessed January 20, 2014).

7. Maxine was a colleague, an inspiration, and a friend. She will be missed. Maxine Harper, *Maxine Harper's Journey of Hope* (Oxford, MS: Lantern Publishing Company, 2011).

Chapter 4

1. Adam Cohen, "Why Is Paddling Still Allowed in Schools?" *Time*, October 1, 2012, http://ideas.time.com/2012/10/01/should-paddling-be-allowed-in-schools/ (accessed January 28, 2013).

2. US Geological Survey, "Geospatial Boundary Data for MS School Districts," US Census and MS Department of Education, 2012. I am indebted to SouthernEcho, a nonprofit organization that released "Mississippi School Districts Corporal Punishment Incidents: 2009–2010 to 2010–2011 School Years," 2012, http://southernecho.org/s/wp-content/uploads/2012/01/01-12-12-map-ms-sch-dist-corp-punshmnt-change-09-10-to-10-11-v7.pdf.

3. I have chosen not to name the teacher, though she gave me

permission to do so. Corporal punishment is a topic that people feel uncomfortable talking about, which, of course, makes it difficult to inquire about.

4. Cohen, "Why Is Paddling Still Allowed in Schools?"

5. Rick Lyman, "In Many Schools, the Paddle Is No Relic," *New York Times*, September 30, 2006, A1.

6. Kids Count, datacenter.kidscount.org.

7. Cohen, "Why Is Paddling Still Allowed in Schools?"

8. Ibid. Among other sources, Cohen is referring to studies such as Murray A. Straus, "Criminogenic Effects of Corporal Punishment by Parents," in *Transnational Criminology Manual*, vol. 1, ed. M. Herzog-Evans and Isabelle Dréan-Rivette, 373–90 (Amsterdam: Wolf Legal Publishing, 2010), and Manuel Gámez-Gaudix, Murray A. Straus, José Antonio Carrobles, Marina J. Muñoz-Rivas, and Carmen Almendros, "Corporal Punishment and Long-Term Behavior Problems: The Moderating Role of Positive Parenting and Psychological Aggression," *Psicothema* 22, no. 5 (2010): 529–36.

9. Murray A. Straus and Emily M. Douglas, "Research on Spanking by Parents: Implications for Public Policy," *Family Psychologist: Bulletin of the Division of Family Psychology* 43, no. 24 (2008): 18–20, 19. In the original passage, the two instances in which I changed the language to "[belief]" were originally "myth." I change them here because "myth" suggests that something was never true. I appreciate that today education is frustrated by corporal punishment, but it is not impossible that long before human beings developed the sophisticated languages we now use, corporal punishment was among the few means to direct behavior.

10. Tracie O. Afifi, Natalie P. Mota, Patricia Dasiewicz, Harriet L. MacMillan, and Jitender Sareen, "Physical Punishment and Mental Disorders: Results from a Nationally Representative US Sample," *Pediatrics* 130, no. 2 (2012): 5, 8.

11. Here I should acknowledge that psychological disorders are subjects of controversy, with definitions that change over time. In addition, several forces can contribute to depression. I would call psychological conditions and descriptions value laden. Nonetheless, I believe I have presented evidence that should raise worries about corporal punishment. In addition, the criticisms I have raised here are centered on what makes sense on behalf of public educational institutions, not for all situations of parenting.

12. Caroline Fabend Bartlett, "You Are What You Serve: Are School Districts Liable for Serving Unhealthy Food and Beverages to Students?," *Seton Hall Law Review* 34, no. 3 (2004): 1053–91.

13. Jacob Axelrad, "Outrage over Adrian Peterson Masks Deeper Acceptance of Corporal Punishment," *Christian Science Monitor*, September 18, 2014, http://www.csmonitor.com/USA/Sports/2014/0918/Outrage-over-Adrian-Peterson-masks-deeper-acceptance-of-corporal-punishment-video.

14. Plato, *Republic*, Book VII, 536e.

15. The Center for Effective Discipline is located in Columbus, Ohio, a state which ended its public schools' widespread use of corporal punishment in the 1980s. The Center's Web site houses many useful resources: http://www.stophitting.com/.

16. Once again, here I am referring to the fact that the federal government is suing Meridian, Mississippi, for allegedly creating a "school-to-prison pipeline." Frieden, "Mississippi Town Sued." The point about Meridian is not specific to corporal punishment, however, but helps to highlight the fact that both corporal punishment and other ineffective forms of discipline are less virtuous than practices identified as "effective" forms of discipline—such as those catalogued by the Center for Effective Discipline, http://www.stophitting.com/.

17. See Eric Thomas Weber, "Mississippians Are Ready for Comprehensive Sex Education," *Science Progress*, February 14, 2012, http://scienceprogress.org/2012/02/mississippians-are

-ready-for-comprehensive-sex-education/. This piece is included in the Appendix, with permission from the editors of *Science Progress* (www.scienceprogress.org).

18. Jennifer J. Frost and Jacqueline Darroch Forrest, "Understanding the Impact of Effective Teenage Pregnancy Prevention Programs," *Family Planning Perspectives* 27, no. 5 (1995): 188–95. See also Rebekah Levine Coley and P. Lindsay Chase-Lansdale, "Adolescent Pregnancy and Parenthood: Recent Evidence and Future Directions," *American Psychologist* 53, no. 2 (February 1998): 152–66. It is worth noting that according to Coley and Chase-Lansdale, the difference between the graduation rates of parents versus nonparents was not large at the time of their study, at least for teenagers who became pregnant before dropping out of school, rather than the reverse. At the same time, they report that "of adolescents who drop out of school either before or shortly after childbirth, only 30 percent return and eventually graduate, about half the rate of nonmother dropouts." Ibid., 155–56.

19. See John B. Jemmott, Loretta S. Jemmott, and Geoffrey T. Fong, "Efficacy of a Theory-Based Abstinence-Only Intervention over 24 Months," *Archives of Pediatric Adolescent Medicine* 164, no. 2 (2010): 152–59. This study has shown a narrow effect on delaying the engagement in sexual intercourse for a select level of students, namely sixth and seventh graders, yet "nearly a quarter of these [students] already had sex by the time they became a part of this study," explains Elizabeth Schroeder, executive director of Answer, a national organization housed at Rutgers University "dedicated to providing and promoting comprehensive sexuality education to young people and the adults who teach them." The key that Schroeder notes from the study is that teaching abstinence is effective as a component of sex education. The most effective results, however, come from a combination targeted comprehensive sex education. Schroeder continues, "Sex education is not about teaching one topic to one age group

and that's it. It has to start at the earliest ages, build upon and reinforce the previous knowledge and skills learned, and evolve as students get older and become more likely to start having sex." See Elizabeth Schroeder, "Comprehensive Sex Ed the Most Effective Approach to Reducing STDs and Pregnancy, Rutgers Experts Say," *Rutgers New Release*, February 3, 2010, http://news.rutgers .edu/medrel/news-releases/2010/01/comprehensive-sex -ed-20100203.

20. Norman A. Constantine, "Converging Evidence Leaves Policy Behind: Sex Education in the United States," *Journal of Adolescent Health* 42, no. 4 (2008): 324–26.

21. Pamela K. Kohler, Lisa E. Manhart, and William E. Lafferty, "Abstinence-Only and Comprehensive Sex Education and the Initiation of Sexual Activity and Teen Pregnancy," *Journal of Adolescent Health* 42, no. 4 (2008): 344–51.

22. This is the publication I mentioned that is included here in the Appendix, "Mississippians Are Ready for Comprehensive Sex Education."

23. Reuters, "Mississippi Schools, with America's Highest Teen Pregnancy Rate, Largely Adopts Abstinence-Only Sex Education," *Huffington Post*, August 26, 2012, http://www.huffington post.com/2012/08/27/feature-mississippi-schoo_n_1831069.html.

Chapter 5

1. Sara Mosle, "Report Card," *New York Times*, August 21, 2011, BR1.

2. Some charters perform better than traditional peers, such as the KIPP schools, and some underperform. See Sam Dillon, "Education Chief to Warn Advocates That Inferior Charter Schools Harm the Effort," *New York Times*, June 22, 2009, A10, and Andrea Billups, "Charter Schools Hit, Miss in New Report:

Limited English, Poverty Students Get Math and Reading Boost," *Washington Times*, June 16, 2009, A5.

3. Geoff Pender, "GOP Split on Charter Bills," *Clarion Ledger*, January 24, 2013, 1A-2A.

4. See my piece, republished in Appendix 6, Eric Thomas Weber, "Try Charter Schools Experiment Where Others Failing," *Clarion Ledger*, March 6, 2010, 9A.

5. Susan Wolf and Mira Browne, "Charter Schools in Arizona Perform Significantly below Their Traditional Public School Peers," *Sanford Report Press Release*, June 15, 2009, http://credo .stanford.edu/reports/statepressreleases/Arizona.pdf. See also Steven Brill, "The Teachers' Unions' Last Stand," *New York Times*, May 23, 2010, M32. Brill writes, "Charter schools are not always better for children. Across the country many are performing badly. But when run well—as most in Harlem and New York's other most-challenged communities appear to be—they can make a huge difference in a child's life."

6. See Kathleen V. Hoover-Dempsey, Joan M. T. Walker, Kathleen P. Jones, and Richard P. Reed, "Teachers Involving Parents (TIP): Results of an In-Service Teacher Education Program for Enhancing Parental Involvement," *Teaching and Teacher Education* 18, no. 7 (October 2002): 843–67, and Mary Murray, Erin Curran, and Denise Zellers, "Building Parent/Professional Partnerships: An Innovative Approach for Teacher Education," *Teacher Educator* 43, no. 2 (2008): 87–108.

7. Associated Press, "KKK Rally at Ole Miss: Klan Outnumbered by Protestors," *Huffington Post*, March 18, 2010, http:// www.huffingtonpost.com/2009/11/21/kkk-rally-at- ole-miss -kla_n_366475.html.

8. Ibid. The "University Creed" reads as follows: "The University of Mississippi is a community of learning dedicated to nurturing excellence in intellectual inquiry and personal character in an open and diverse environment. As a voluntary member

of this community: I believe in respect for the dignity of each person; I believe in fairness and civility; I believe in personal and professional integrity; I believe in academic honesty; I believe in academic freedom; I believe in good stewardship of our resources; I pledge to uphold these values and encourage others to follow my example." See "University Creed," University of Mississippi, http://www.olemiss.edu/info/creed.html (accessed March 11, 2013). The university adopted the creed in 2003. Leslie Banahan, ed., *The Ole Miss Experience: First Year Experience Text* (Taylor, MS: Nautilus Publishing Company, 2012), 155.

9. Nancy MacLean, *Behind the Mask of Chivalry: The Making of the Second Ku Klux Klan* (New York: Oxford University Press, 1994), 127.

10. Geoffrey Brewer, "Snakes Top List of Americans' Fears," *Gallup*, March 19, 2001, http://www.gallup.com/poll/1891/snakes-top-list-americans-fears.aspx.

11. Hunter Nicholson, "Race and the Greek System at Ole Miss," *Daily Mississippian*, September 20, 2011, 2–3, and at http://archive.thedmonline.com/article/race-and-greek-system -ole-miss-0 (accessed January 28, 2013).

12. Leslie Banahan and K. B. Melear, co-chairs, *Incident Review Committee: Public Report* (Oxford: University Press of Mississippi, January 25, 2013).

13. Lexi Thoman, "The Ghosts of Ole Miss Are Far from Dead," *Daily Mississippian*, November 8, 2012, 3, http://archive.thed monline.com/article/ghosts-ole-miss-are-far-dead (accessed January 28, 2013.

14. Ibid.

Chapter 6

1. Plato, *Republic*, Book V, 462b.

2. It is worth noting that Plato would label Lee a timocrat because of this line—a lover of honor above all else.

3. Letter from Robert E. Lee to G. W. P. Custis (Jan. 23, 1861). I encountered the letter in Alan T. Nolan, *Lee Considered: General Robert E. Lee and Civil War History* (Chapel Hill, NC: University of North Carolina Press, 1996), 34–35.

4. Plato, *Republic*, Book IV, 422e–423a.

5. It reads, "The powers not delegated to the United States by the Constitution, nor prohibited by it to the States, are reserved to the States respectively, or to the people." Tenth Amendment, *Constitution of the United States of America.*

6. Kenneth T. Andrews, "Movement-Counter Movement Dynamics and the Emergence of New Institutions: The Case of 'White Flight' Schools in Mississippi," *Social Forces* 80, no. 3 (March 2002): 911. The data about the number of schools is on page 912.

7. Such trends have been well documented for many years. For example, see Christine H. Rossell, "School Desegregation and White Flight," *Political Science Quarterly* 90, no. 4 (Winter 1975–1976): 675–95.

8. Elizabeth Anderson, *The Imperative of Integration* (Princeton, NJ: Princeton University Press, 2010), ix.

9. Derrick A. Bell Jr., "Brown v. Board of Education and the Interest-Convergence Dilemma," *Harvard Law Review* 93, no. 3 (January 1980): 518–33.

10. Ibid., 533.

11. I should qualify here that "self-interested" for a democratic leader must mean "self" in an expansive sense, not in some atomistic, "man-is-an-island" sense.

12. Oddly enough, some have tried to take up this phrase in an effort that seems a great deal more like the notion that resembles "some rising boats raise the tide." In particular, Jim Pinkerton argues for lowering corporate taxes, which he suggests will then

improve the lives of the middle class, and that thus everyone will benefit from the risen tide. Pinkerton gets the metaphor backward, it seems. See Jim Pinkerton, "Rising Tide for the American People: Prosperity Goes Up as Corporate Tax Goes Down," *Washington Times*, December 9, 2011, B1.

13. Gene Sperling, "Rising-Tide Economics," *Democracy: A Journal of Ideas* 6 (Fall 2007): 61–73.

14. Elizabeth Anderson, "Why Racial Integration Remains an Imperative," *Poverty and Race* 20, no. 4 (2011): 1–19.

15. Jane Dailey, "Sex, Segregation, and the Sacred after *Brown*," *Journal of American History* 91, no. 1 (2004): 119–44.

16. Ibid., 119–20.

17. Aaron J. Leichman, "Survey: Nation's 'Most Religious' Population in Mississippi," *Christian Post*, December 22, 2009, http://www.christianpost.com/news/42383/ (accessed January 28, 2013).

18. I acknowledge that Plato referred to the ideal city and did not make use of a concept of a "state." I mean here only the public entity.

19. John Blake, "Why Sunday Morning Remains America's Most Segregated Hour," *CNN Religion Blog*, October 6, 2010, http://religion.blogs.cnn.com/2010/10/06/why-sunday-morning -remains-americas-most-segregated-hour/.

20. Ed Pilkington, "United States: Black Couple's Wedding Ruined by Churchgoers," *The Guardian* (London), July 30, 2012, 14.

21. Ibid.

22. I qualify here that this is true when it comes to race. In reference to other matters, such as the importance of the insights of the sciences, people in Mississippi are often united on religious grounds in their rejection of what the best science teaches. Facts about what is the most effective sex education are dismissed and those about evolution and physical sciences are treated as if they

were efforts to trick people. To be sure, religious practices can motivate the best in people, but at one time in American history, they also motivated witch hunts and other forms of oppression.

23. In American history this was not always the case. See Thornton Stringfellow, *Scriptural and Statistical Views in Favor of Slavery* (Richmond, VA: J. W. Randolph, 1865).

24. The emphasis added here means to distinguish religions from what Dewey called the religious aspect of experience, hence religions versus the religious. John Dewey, *A Common Faith* (New Haven, CT: Yale University Press, 1934), 1.

25. For a few examples, see Gerald L. Zelizer, "Where Did We Come From? (And What Can We Teach Our Kids?)," *USA Today*, February 7, 2005, 15A, and Peter Whoriskey, "Evangelical Democrat Stirs the Pot in Miss.," *Washington Post*, November 5, 2007, A3.

26. In the latter categories, we can place authors like Sigmund Freud and Bertrand Russell. See Sigmund Freud, *Civilization and Its Discontents* (New York: W. W. Norton, 1989), and Bertrand Russell, *Religion and Science* (New York: Oxford University Press, 1997).

27. For a rich look at Dewey's appreciation of spiritual values, see Larry A. Hickman, "John Dewey's Spiritual Values," *Dewey's Enduring Impact: Essays on America's Philosopher*, ed. John Shook and Paul Kurtz (Albany, NY: Prometheus Books, 2011), 193–203.

28. Cornel West, *Prophecy Deliverance! An Afro-American Revolutionary Christianity* (Philadelphia: Westminster Press, 1982). West presents a rich and provocative Christian, revolutionary Marxism. His proposal is not intended to divide people, but to unite all people in understanding and appreciation of suffering, which must be alleviated, according to Christian doctrine.

29. Cornel West, *Hope on a Tightrope* (New York: Smiley Books, 2008), 198–99.

Chapter 7

1. Again, I am referring to Carr, "In Southern Towns, 'Segregation Academies' Are Still Going Strong."

2. Ibid.

3. Ibid.

4. Ibid.

5. ACT, Inc., "ACT Profile Report—State: Graduating Class 2012, Mississippi," *The ACT*, 2012, 8–9, http://www.act.org/news room/data/2012/pdf/profile/ Mississippi.pdf.

6. Marc Mauer and Ryan S. King, *Uneven Justice: State Rates of Incarceration by Race and Ethnicity* (Washington, DC: The Sentencing Project, July 2007), 11, http://www.sentencingproject. org/doc/publications/rd_stateratesofincbyraceandethnicity.pdf.

7. Robert Nozick, *Anarchy, State and Utopia* (New York: Basic Books, 1974).

8. Nozick's idea here also misses the fact that patterns are not only the product of individuals' free interactions. They are also the intentional consequences of public policy, whereby crimes committed by poor people or persons of minority groups are prosecuted and sentenced in ways far harsher than those of the dominant group, as in the differential sentencing of crack and cocaine. West proclaims, "We have to recognize that there is a radical continuity between the killing fields of the plantations, the bodies hanging from the trees, police brutality, the prison-industrial complex, and the Superdome in New Orleans after Hurricane Katrina." West, *Hope on a Tightrope*, 45. Also, in a study controlling for "legally relevant factors, socioeconomic factors, and legal contextual factors, it was found that blacks convicted of cocaine offenses and Hispanics convicted of cocaine and marijuana offenses were sentenced more harshly than white offenders." See Christopher G. Hebert, "Sentencing Outcomes of Black,

Hispanic, and White Males Convicted Under Federal Sentencing Guidelines," *Criminal Justice Review* 22, no. 2 (1997): 133–56. Nozick's notion that unintended patterns are not the areas in which to look for justice discounts the possibility that intentions can be very old and tacit, and even when unintentional, result in grossly unfair differentials of sentencing for the same crime.

9. John Stackhouse, "Pilgrims Meet Death at Hindu Shrines: Sixty Die in Stampedes7 at Temple," *Globe and Mail* (Toronto), July 16, 1996, A1. Am7ong the injured and dead, five children were trampled or suffocated when it turned out that a bridge had been damaged in a flood, leaving only a single remaining structure on the river Ganges. Pushes and shoves turned to panic, yielding the sixty deaths in question. Patterns of individual action can in some cases be predicted and redirected with good leadership, even if this was not true in the case cited here.

10. Carr, "In Southern Towns, 'Segregation Academies' Are Still Going Strong."

11. To be sure, "tokenism" is itself a force of racism in communities and organizations that feature very little diversity and therefore use their few persons of non-European descent not as equal members of their group, but as badges which highlight the fact that they are not entirely white-only institutions. See Yolanda Flores Niemann, "The Making of a Token: A Case Study of Stereotype Threat, Stigma, Racism, and Tokenism in Academe," *Frontiers: A Journal of Women Studies* 20, no. 1 (1999): 111–34.

12. Mullins, *Building Consensus*.

13. Of course financial barriers to access remain and are explicit, but apply to all who cannot afford relevant costs.

14. According to the Admissions Office at the University of Mississippi, http://www.olemiss.edu/admissions/fap.html.

15. ACT, Inc., "ACT Profile Report—State: Graduating Class 2012, Mississippi,"

16. Justice Department FBI Press Release, "Mississippi Man

Pleads Guilty to Conspiring to Commit Hate Crimes against African-Americans in Jackson," Justice Department Documents and Publications, January 3, 2013.

17. Associated Press, "3 Plead Guilty to Hate Crimes in Mississippi Murder," *CBS News*, March 23, 2012, http://www.cbsnews.com/8301-201_162-57403017/, and Dalina Castellanos, "Matthew Shepard Act Applied in Mississippi Hate Crime," *Los Angeles Times*, March 24, 2012, http://articles.latimes.com/2012/mar/24/nation/la-na-nn-three-charged-and-sentenced-in- mississippi-hate-crime-20120323.

18. Ibid.

19. Justice Department, "Mississippi Man Pleads Guilty."

20. Ibid.

21. Associated Press, "3 Plead Guilty."

22. The phrase is attributed to Martin Luther King Jr. Blake, "Why Sunday Morning Remains America's Most Segregated Hour."

23. Phil West, "Mississippi Governor Zooms in on Education during State of the State Speech," *Commercial Appeal* (Memphis) January 22, 2013, http://www.commercialappeal.com/ news/2013/jan/22/mississippi-governor-zooms-in-on-education-state/.

Chapter 8

1. John Dewey, *Experience and Nature*, in *The Collected Works of John Dewey, The Later Works*, vol. 1, *1925*, ed. Jo Ann Boydston (Carbondale: Southern Illinois University–Carbondale, 2008), 132.

2. Again, from Peter Whoriskey, "By the Mississippi Delta."

3. "2014-15 MAEP Salary Schedule, MS Code Section 37-19-7," School Financial Services, Mississippi Department of Education, http://www.mde.k12.ms.us/docs/school-financial-services-library/teacher-salary-schedule.pdf.

4. "Critical Shortage Areas by County," Mississippi Department of Education, http://www.mde.k12.ms.us/teacher-center/critical-shortage-areas/critical-shortage-areas-by-county.

5. Mississippi Economic Policy Center, "The Nuts and Bolts of the Mississippi Budget: A Taxpayer's Guide to the Mississippi Budget," [Report] Hope Enterprise Corporation and the Mississippi Economic Policy Center, Jackson, MS, 2012, http://mepconline.org/images/admin/pdfs/179_26933_2012%20Budget%20&%20Tax%20WEB.pdf. Editorial, "Reeves Proposes More Income Tax Cuts, Bumping Total to $550M," *Mississippi Business Journal*, March 16, 2015, http://msbusiness.com/businessblog/2015/03/16/reeves-proposes-more-income-tax-cuts-bumping-total-to-550m/.

6. This line was related on the Facebook page run by the William Winter Institute for Racial Reconciliation, October 15, 2014, https://www.facebook.com/pages/William-Winter-Institute-for-Racial-Reconciliation/295860466710.

7. William J. Bennett, *The Book of Virtues: A Treasury of Great Moral Stories* (New York: Simon and Schuster, 1996), and William J. Bennett, *The Children's Book of Virtues* (New York: Simon and Schuster, 1995).

8. Benjamin Franklin, *Autobiography* (1793; New York: P. F. Collier and Son Company, 2012), 87.

9. Amy-Ellen Duke and Evelyn Ganzglass, *Strengthening State Adult Education Policies for Low-Skilled Workers* (Chevy Chase, MD: Working Poor Families Project, Summer 2007), 1–8, http://www.workingpoorfamilies.org/pdfs/PB_adult_education.pdf.

10. See Eric Thomas Weber, "Teachers Offer Hope," included here as Appendix 5.

11. One of the most impressive illustrations of students' will to serve Mississippi that I have seen is evident in the yearly "Big Event," which I have witnessed at the University of Mississippi. The 2013 event pulled in 2,700 students to volunteer on the Big

Event weekend. Note that the local population of Oxford, Mississippi, is approximately 20,000 according to the US Census. See Melanie Addington, "Big Event Continues to Grow," *Oxford Eagle*, January 22, 2013, 2.

12. I am thinking here of my dear friend, the Reverend Julius Minor, who passed away in 2012. "Julius Minor," *Toledo Blade* (obituary), September 28, 2012, http://www.legacy.com/obituar ies/toledoblade/obituary.aspx?pid=160149085 (accessed March 22, 2013).

13. Jan Hoffman, "Does 8th-Grade Pomp Fit the Circumstance," *New York Times*, June 22, 2008, ST1, http://www.nytimes .com/2008/06/22/fashion/22grad.html.

14. See, for example, Hank Bounds, J. Martez Hill, and Sheril R. Smith, "State Dropout Prevention Plan, 2007–2019," Mississippi Department of Education, Jackson, 2007, http://archive .hattiesburgamerican.com/assets/pdf/DB10811959.PDF.

15. Johns Hopkins Researchers, "Dropout Factories." Notice also that Mississippi spent $9,708 per pupil in 2009, compared with Iowa's $12,007. Simply to match Iowa's spending could help, but to catch up should be expected to take more, particularly in addressing the needs of impoverished people. See the Annie E. Casey Foundation, "Data across States," Kids Count Data Center, 2009, http:// datacenter.kidscount.org/data/acrossstates/Rank ings.aspx?ind=5199 (accessed March 22, 2013).

16. Eric Thomas Weber, "Teachers Offer Hope."

Appendix 2

1. In the original version of this article, I had the added qualification that Brent was "self-described as a person from a modest financial background." He let me know that this was not an accurate representation of how he thinks of himself and must have been drawn from a misinterpretation or some other mistake. He was kind and understanding about my error.

BIBLIOGRAPHY

"2014–15 MAEP Salary Schedule, MS Code Section 37-19-7,"
School Financial Services, Mississippi Department of Education. http://www.mde.k12.ms.us/docs/school-financial-servic
es-library/teacher-salary-schedule.pdf.

Abrams, Lisa M., Joseph J. Pedulla, and George F. Madaus.
"Views from the Classroom: Teachers' Opinions of Statewide
Testing Programs." *Theory Into Practice* 42, no. 1 (Winter
2003): 18–29.

Abu-nasr, Donna. "Saudi Women Get in the Driver's Seat; Flout
Licence Ban." *National Post* (Toronto). June 18, 2011, A23.

ACT, Inc. "2012 ACT National and State Scores." *The ACT*, 2012.
http://www.act.org/newsroom/data/2012/states.html.

——. "Compare ACT & SAT Scores." June 2008. http://www
.act.org/solutions/college-career-readiness/compare-act-sat/.

——. "The Condition of College and Career Readiness, 2012:
Mississippi." *ACT.org*, 2012. http://www.act.org/newsroom/
data/2012/states/pdf/Mississippi.pdf.

——. "Graduating Class 2012: National." *ACT Profile Report—
National*, 2012. http://www.act.org/newsroom/data/2012/pdf/
profile/National2012.pdf.

Addington, Melanie. "Big Event Continues to Grow." *Oxford
Eagle*, January 22, 2013, 2.

Adorno, T. W. "Democratic Leadership and Mass Manipulation."
In *Studies in Leadership: Leadership and Democratic Action*.
Edited by A. W. Gouldner, 418–35. New York: Russell & Rus-
sell, 1950.

Afifi, Tracie O., Natalie P. Mota, Patricia Dasiewicz, Harriet L.

MacMillan, and Jitender Sareen, "Physical Punishment and Mental Disorders: Results from a Nationally Representative US Sample." *Pediatrics* 130, no. 2 (2012): 1–9.

Allen, Douglas and Murray Young. "From Tour Guide to Teacher: Deepening Cross-Cultural Competence through International Experience–Based Education." *Journal of Management Education* 21, no. 2 (1997): 168–89.

Allen, Nick. "Mississippi Church Refuses to Marry Black Couple." *Daily Telegraph* (Chatham, Kent, UK), July 30, 2012, 15.

Alliance for Excellent Education. "Understanding High School Graduation Rates in Mississippi." July 2009. http://www.all4ed.org/files/Mississippi_wc.pdf

Al-Yousif, Yousif Khalifa. "Exports and Economic Growth: Some Empirical Evidence from the Arab Gulf Countries." *Applied Economics* 29, no. 6 (1997): 693–97.

Anderson, Elizabeth. *The Imperative of Integration*. Princeton, NJ: Princeton University Press, 2010.

———. "Why Racial Integration Remains an Imperative." *Poverty and Race* 20, no. 4 (2011): 1–19.

Andrews, Kenneth T. "Movement–Countermovement Dynamics and the Emergence of New Institutions: The Case of 'White Flight' Schools in Mississippi." *Social Forces* 80, no. 3 (2002): 911–936.

Annie E. Casey Foundation, The. "Kids Count Data Book: State Trends in Child Well-Being, 2012." http://www.kidscount.org.

Antonakis, John, Anna T. Cianciolo, and Robert J. Sternberg, eds., *The Nature of Leadership*. Thousand Oaks, CA: Sage Press, 2004.

Arendt, Hannah. *On Violence*. New York: Harcourt Brace, 1970.

Aristotle. *The Nicomachean Ethics*. Trans. David Ross. Ed. John L. Ackrill, and James O. Urmson. New York: Oxford University Press, 1998.

———. *The Politics*. Trans. Ernest Barker. Ed. R. F. Stalley. New York: Oxford University Press, 2009.

Asser, Seth M., and Rita Swan. "Child Fatalities from Religion-Motivated Medical Neglect." *Pediatrics* 101, no. 4 (1998): 625–29.

Associated Press. "3 Plead Guilty to Hate Crimes in Mississippi Murder." *CBS News*. March 23, 2012. http://www.cbsnews .com/8301-201_162-57403017/.

———. "Interracial Couple Denied Marriage License by Louisiana Justice of the Peace." *Huffington Post*. March 18, 2010. http:// www.huffingtonpost.com/2009/10/15/interracial-couple -denied_n_322784.html.

———. "KKK Rally at Ole Miss: Klan Outnumbered by Protestors." *Huffington Post*. March 18, 2010. http://www.huffing tonpost.com/2009/11/21/kkk-rally-at-ole-miss-kla_n_366475 .html.

———. "More Mississippi Students Unprepared to Start College." *WTVA, NBC News Affiliate*. June 3, 2012. http://www .wtva.com/news/local/story/More-Mississippi-students-un prepared-to-start/tbHxrmht9oe9fnaTGRP61g.cspx.

Aurelius, Marcus. *Meditations*. New York: Penguin Classics, 2006.

Axelrad, Jacob. "Outrage over Adrian Peterson Masks Deeper Acceptance of Corporal Punishment." *Christian Science Monitor*, September 18, 2014. http://www.csmonitor.com/USA/ Sports/2014/0918/Outrage-over-Adrian-Peterson-masks -deeper-acceptance-of-corporal-punishment-video.

Babbitt, Irving. *Democracy and Leadership*. Indianapolis, IN: Liberty Fund, 1979.

Banahan, Leslie, ed. *The Ole Miss Experience: First Year Experience Text*. Taylor, MS: Nautilus Publishing, 2012.

Banahan, Leslie, and K. B. Melear. *Incident Review Committee: Public Report*. Oxford: University Press of Mississippi, 2013.

Bartlett, Caroline Fabend. "You Are What You Serve: Are School Districts Liable for Serving Unhealthy Food and Beverages to Students?" *Seton Hall Law Review* 34, no. 3 (2004): 1053–91.

Bass, Bernard M. "From Transactional to Transformational Leadership: Learning to Share the Vision." *Organizational Dynamics* 18, no. 3 (1990): 19–31.

Bass, Bernard M., ed. *Bass & Stogdill's Handbook of Leadership: Theory, Research, and Managerial Applications.* 3rd ed. New York: Macmillan, 1990.

Bass, S. Jonathan. *Blessed Are the Peacemakers: Martin Luther King Jr., Eight White Religious Leaders, and the "Letter from Birmingham Jail."* Baton Rouge, LA: Louisiana State University Press, 2001.

Batker, David K., and John de Graaf. *What's the Economy For, Anyway?* New York: Bloomsbury Press, 2011.

Baumeister, Roy F., and Brad J. Bushman. *Social Psychology and Human Nature.* Belmont, CA: Wadsworth Publishing, 2011.

Bell, Derrick A., Jr. "Brown v. Board of Education and the Interest-Convergence Dilemma." *Harvard Law Review* 93, no. 3 (January 1980): 518–33.

Bennett, William J. *The Book of Virtues: A Treasury of Great Moral Stories.* New York: Simon and Schuster, 1996.

———. *The Children's Book of Virtues.* New York: Simon and Schuster, 1995.

Berlin, Isaiah. *Two Concepts of Liberty.* Oxford: Clarendon Press, 1958.

Berrett, Dan. "Philosophers Put Their Minds to Expanding Their Role in Public Affairs." *Chronicle of Higher Education* 58, no. 17 (December 11, 2011): A16–17.

Biesta, Gert J. J., and Siebren Miedema. "Dewey in Europe: A Case Study on the International Dimensions of the Turn-of-the-Century Educational Reform." *American Journal of Education* 105, no. 1 (1996): 1–26.

Billups, Andrea. "Charter Schools Hit, Miss in New Report: Limited English, Poverty Students Get Math and Reading Boost." *Washington Times*, June 16, 2009, A5.

Blackwell, Lisa S., Kali H. Trzesniewski, and Carol Sorich Dweck. "Implicit Theories of Intelligence Predict Achievement across an Adolescent Transition: A Longitudinal Study and an Intervention." *Child Development* 78, no. 1 (2007): 246–63.

Blake, John. "Why Sunday Morning Remains America's Most Segregated Hour." *CNN Religion Blog*. October 6, 2010. http://religion.blogs.cnn.com/2010/10/06/why-sunday-morning -remains-americas-most-segregated-hour/.

Blanchard, Kenneth, and Spencer Johnson. *The One Minute Manager*. New York: William Morrow, 1982.

Bloomberg Bureau of National Affairs (BNA). "Most and Least Taxing States 2012." *Bloomberg.com*. April 13, 2012. http://www.bloomberg.com/money-gallery/2011-09-14/most-least -taxing-states.html.

Bounds, Hank, J. Martez Hill, and Sheril R. Smith. "State Dropout Prevention Plan, 2007–2019." Mississippi Department of Education. Jackson, MS, 2007. http://archive.hattiesbur gamerican.com/assets/pdf/DB10811959.PDF.

Brewer, Geoffrey. "Snakes Top List of Americans' Fears." *Gallup*, March 19, 2001. http://www.gallup.com/poll/1891/snakes-top -list-americans-fears.aspx.

Brill, Steven. "The Teachers' Unions' Last Stand." *New York Times*, May 23, 2010, M32.

Brown, Robbie. "Anti-Obama Protest at Ole Miss Turns Unruly." *New York Times*, November 7, 2012, P9.

"Bullying, a Deadly Sin." (Editorial). *America: The National Catholic Review* 754, November 8, 2010. http://americamaga zine.org/issue/754/editorial/bullying-deadly-sin.

Burns, James McGregor. *Leadership*. New York: Harper Torchbooks, 1979.

————. *Transforming Leadership: A New Pursuit of Happiness.* New York: Grove Press, 2003.

Carr, Sarah. "In Southern Towns, 'Segregation Academies' Are Still Going Strong." *The Atlantic*, December 13, 2012. http://www.theatlantic.com/national/archive/2012/12/in-southern -towns-segregation-academies-are-still-going-strong/266207/.

Castellanos, Dalina. "Matthew Shepard Act Applied in Mississippi Hate Crime." *Los Angeles Times*, March 24, 2012. http://articles.latimes.com/2012/mar/24/nation/la-na-nn-three -charged-and-sentenced-in-mississippi-hate-crime-20120323.

Cataldi, Emily Forrest, Caitlin Green, Robin Henke, Terry Lew et al. "2008–09 Baccalaureate and Beyond Longitudinal Study: First Look." *National Center for Education Statistics, NCES 2011–236.* Washington, DC: US Department of Education, 2011. http://nces.ed.gov/pubs2011/2011236.pdf.

Center for Public Leadership at the John F. Kennedy School of Government. "Confidence in Leadership Survey, September 2008." Retrieved February 8, 2012, from the iPOLL Databank. The Roper Center for Public Opinion Research. University of Connecticut.

Choi, Seung-Whan. "Democratic Leadership: The Lessons of Exemplary Models for Democratic Governance." *International Journal of Leadership Studies* 2, no. 3 (2007): 243–62.

Cialdini, Robert B. *Influence: The Psychology of Persuasion.* New York: HarperCollins, 2007.

Ciulla, Joanne, ed. *Ethics: The Heart of Leadership.* Westport, CT: Praeger, 2004.

Cohen, Adam. "Why Is Paddling Still Allowed in Schools?" *Time*, October 1, 2012. http://ideas.time.com/2012/10/01/should -paddling-be-allowed-in-schools/.

Coley, Rebekah Levine, and P. Lindsay Chase-Lansdale. "Adolescent Pregnancy and Parenthood: Recent Evidence and Future

Directions." *American Psychologist* 53, no. 2 (February 1998): 152–66.

Collins, Jim. *Good to Great*. New York: HarperCollins, 2001.

———. *Good to Great in the Social Sectors: Why Business Thinking Is Not the Answer*. New York: HarperCollins, 2005.

"community, n." OED Online. March 2013. Oxford University Press.

Confucius. *The Analects*. New York: Penguin Books, 1979.

Constantine, Norman A. "Converging Evidence Leaves Policy Behind: Sex Education in the United States." *Journal of Adolescent Health* 42, no. 4 (2008): 324–26.

Constitution of the United States of America.

Couto, Richard A., ed. *Political and Civic Leadership: A Reference Handbook*. Thousand Oaks, CA: SAGE Publications, 2010.

Covey, Stephen R. *The 7 Habits of Highly Effective People*. New York: Simon and Schuster, 1989.

Cutler, David M., and Adriana Lleras-Muney. "Education and Health: Evaluating Theories and Evidence." National Bureau of Economic Research, Working Paper Series. June 2006. http://www.nber.org/papers/w12352.

Dahl, Robert. *Democracy and Its Critics*. New Haven, CT: Yale University Press, 1991.

Dailey, Jane. "Sex, Segregation, and the Sacred after Brown." *Journal of American History* 91, no. 1 (2004): 119–44.

Dattel, Eugene R. "Cotton in a Global Economy: Mississippi (1800–1860)." *Mississippi History Now*. http://mshistorynow.mdah.state.ms.us/articles/161/cotton-in-a-global-economy-mississippi-1800-1860.

Deal, Terrence E., and Kent D. Peterson. *Shaping School Culture: The Heart of Leadership*. San Francisco: Jossey-Bass, 1999.

Dewey, John. *Art as Experience*. In *The Collected Works of John Dewey, The Later Works*. Vol. 10. Edited by Jo Ann Boydston. Carbondale: Southern Illinois University Press, 1991.

———. *A Common Faith*. New Haven, CT: Yale University Press, 1934.

———. "Attacks Wage Disparity." *The Collected Works of John Dewey, The Later Works.* Vol. 5, *1929–1930.* Edited by Jo Ann Boydston. 431. Carbondale: Southern Illinois University Press, 1988.

———. "Between Two Worlds." In *The Collected Works of John Dewey, The Later Works.* Vol. 17. Edited by Jo Ann Boydston. Carbondale: Southern Illinois University Press, 1991.

———. *Construction and Criticism.* In *The Collected Works of John Dewey, The Later Works.* Vol. 5. Edited by Jo Ann Boydston, 125–44. Carbondale: Southern Illinois University Press, 1984.

———. "Contributions to a Cyclopedia of Education: Democracy and Education." In *The Collected Works of John Dewey, The Middle Works.* Vol. 6, *1910–1911.* Edited by Jo Ann Boydston, 357–467. Carbondale: Southern Illinois University Carbondale, 1976.

———. "Creative Democracy—The Task Before Us." In *The Collected Works of John Dewey, Later Works.* Vol. 14. Edited by Jo Ann Boydston. Carbondale: Southern Illinois University Press, 1988.

———. "Democracy Is Radical." In *The Collected Works of John Dewey, Later Works.* Vol. 11. Edited by Jo Ann Boydston, 296–99. Carbondale: Southern Illinois University Press, 1987.

———. *Democracy and Education.* In *The Middle Works of John Dewey.* Vol. 9. Edited by Jo Ann Boydston. Carbondale: Southern Illinois University Press, 2008.

———. "Democracy and Educational Administration." In *The Collected Works of John Dewey: The Later Works.* Vol. 11. Edited by Jo Ann Boydston, 217–26. Carbondale: Southern Illinois University Press, 1991.

———. "Democracy Is Radical *and* Creative Democracy: The

Task before Us." In *The Essential Dewey*. Vol. 1. Edited by
Larry A. Hickman and Thomas M. Alexander, 337–43. Bloomington: Indiana University Press, 1998.

———. "The Development of American Pragmatism." In *The Collected Works of John Dewey, Later Works*. Vol. 2, *1925–1927*.
Edited by Jo Ann Boydston, 3–21. Carbondale: Southern Illinois University Press, 1984.

———. "The Direction of Education." In *The Collected Works
of John Dewey, The Later Works*. Vol. 3. Edited by Jo Ann
Boydston, 252–53. Carbondale: Southern Illinois University
Press, 1984. First published in *School and Society* 27 (April 28,
1928): 493–97.

———. "The Economic Situation: A Challenge to Education."
The Collected Works of John Dewey, The Later Works. Vol. 6.
Edited by Jo Ann Boydston, 123–31. Carbondale: Southern
Illinois University Press, 1985.

———. "Ethical Principles Underlying Education." In *The Collected Works of John Dewey, The Early Works*. Vol. 5. Edited
by Jo Ann Boydston, 54–83. Carbondale: Southern Illinois
University Press, 1972.

———. *Experience and Nature*. In *The Collected Works ofJohn
Dewey, The Later Works*. Vol. 1. Edited by Jo Ann Boydston.
Carbondale: Southern Illinois University Press, 1988.

———. "Force and Coercion." In *The Collected Works of John
Dewey, The Middle Works*. Vol. 10. Edited by Jo Ann Boydston,
244–52. Carbondale: Southern Illinois University Press, 1980.

———. "From Absolutism to Experimentalism." In *The Collected
Works of John Dewey, The Later Works*. Vol. 5, *1929–1930*.
Edited by Jo Ann Boydston, 147–60. Carbondale: Southern
Illinois University Press, 1988.

———. *Human Nature and Conduct*. In *The Collected Works
of John Dewey, The Middle Works*. Vol. 14. Edited by Jo Ann

Boydston. Carbondale: Southern Illinois University Press, 1983.

———. "The Inclusive Philosophic Idea." In *The Collected Works of John Dewey, The Later Works*. Vol. 3, *1927–1928*. Edited by Jo Ann Boydston, 41–54. Carbondale: Southern Illinois University, 1981.

———. "Individuality, Equality, and Superiority." In *The Collected Works of John Dewey, The Middle Works*. Vol. 13. Edited by Jo Ann Boydston, 296–97. Carbondale: Southern Illinois University Press, 1983. First published in *New Republic* 33 (1922): 61–63.

———. "Philosophy and Democracy." In *The Collected Works of John Dewey, The Middle Works*. Vol. 11. Edited by Jo Ann Boydston, 41–53. Carbondale: Southern Illinois University Press, 1982.

———. "The Prospects of the Liberal College." In *The Collected Works of John Dewey: The Middle Works*. Vol. 15. Edited by Jo Ann Boydston, 200–204. Carbondale: Southern Illinois University Press, 1983.

———. *The Public and Its Problems*. In *The Collected Works of John Dewey, The Later Works*. Vol. 2. Edited by Jo Ann Boydston. Carbondale: Southern Illinois University Press, 1984.

———. *The Quest for Certainty*. In *The Collected Works of John Dewey, The Later Works*. Vol. 4, *1929*. Edited by Jo Ann Boydston. Carbondale: Southern Illinois University Press, 1984.

———. "The Reflex Arc Concept in Psychology." *Psychological Review* 3, no. 4 (July 1896): 357–70.

———. "Social Absolutism." In *The Collected Works of John Dewey, The Middle Works*. Vol. 13. Edited by Jo Ann Boydston, 311–16. Carbondale: Southern Illinois University Press, 1983.

———. "Virtue and the Virtues." In *The Study of Ethics: A Sylla-*

bus. In *The Collected Works of John Dewey: The Early Works.* Vol. 4. Edited by Jo Ann Boydston, 351–62. Carbondale: Southern Illinois University Press, 1975.

———. "What Is It All About?" In *The Collected Works of John Dewey, The Later Works.* Vol. 6. Edited by Jo Ann Boydston, 330–34. Carbondale: Southern Illinois University Press, 1985.

Dewey, John, and James Tufts. *Ethics* (1908). In *The Collected Works of John Dewey, The Middle Works.* Vol. 5. Edited by Jo Ann Boydston. Carbondale: Southern Illinois University Carbondale, 1978.

———. *Ethics* (1932). In *The Collected Works of John Dewey, The Later Works.* Vol. 7, *1932*. Edited by Jo Ann Boydston. Carbondale: Southern Illinois University Press, 1989.

Diestler, Sherry. *Becoming a Critical Thinker.* 5th ed. Upper Saddle River, NJ: Pearson, 2009.

Dillin, John. "Is Morality in Decline?" *Christian Science Monitor*, December 16, 1998, 1.

Dillon, Sam. "Education Chief to Warn Advocates That Inferior Charter Schools Harm the Effort." *New York Times*, June 22, 2009, A10.

———. "States' Data Obscure How Few Finish High School." *New York Times*, March 20, 2008, A1.

Douglass, Frederick. "'The Meaning of the Fourth of July for the Negro,' Speech at Rochester, NY, July 5, 1852." In *Frederick Douglass: Selected Speeches and Writings.* Edited by Philip S. Foner, 188–206. Chicago: Lawrence Hill Books, 1999.

Downey, Maureen. "Feds Release New High School Grad Data Using Common Yard Stick." *Atlanta Journal-Constitution* for the *AJC Get Schooled Blog*, November 26, 2012. http://blogs.ajc.com/get-schooled-blog/2012/11/26/.

Dubow, Eric F., and Maria F. Ippolito. "Effects of Poverty and Quality of the Home Environment on Changes in the Academic and Behavioral Adjustment of Elementary School-Age

Children." *Journal of Clinical Child Psychology* 23, no. 4 (1994): 401–12.

Duke, Amy-Ellen, and Evelyn Ganzglass. *Strengthening State Adult Education Policies for Low-Skilled Workers.* Chevy Chase, MD: Working Poor Families Project, Summer 2007. http://www.workingpoorfamilies.org/pdfs/PB_adult_educa tion.pdf.

Dweck, Carol S. *Mindset.* New York: Random House, 2006.

Editorial. "Reeves Proposes More Income Tax Cuts, Bumping Total to $550M." *Mississippi Business Journal,* March 16, 2015. http://msbusiness.com/businessblog/2015/03/16/reeves-pro poses-more-income-tax-cuts-bumping-total-to-550m/.

Editorial. "The Two Points of View on Education." *New York Times,* March 18, 1923, 3.

Edmonson III, Henry T. *John Dewey and the Decline of American Education.* Wilmington, DE: ISI Books, 2006.

Edsall, Thomas Byrne. "Perils of America's Deep Political Rift." *Washington Post,* February 5, 2012, B6.

Enomoto, Ernestine K., and Bruce H. Kramer. *Leading through the Quagmire: Ethical Foundations, Critical Methods, and Practical Applications for School Leadership.* Lanham, MD: Rowman and Littlefield Education, 2007.

Epictetus. *The Handbook (The Encheiridion).* Translated by Nicholas White. Indianapolis, IN: Hackett Publishing, 1983.

Esfahani, Emily. "Libertarian Logic." *Washington Times,* October 17, 2012, C10.

Faulkner, William. *Requiem for a Nun.* 1950; New York: Vintage Press, 2011.

Fiorina, Morris P., and Samuel J. Abrams. "Political Polarization in the American Public." *Annual Review of Political Science* 11 (June 2008): 563–88.

Foner, Philip S., ed. *Frederick Douglass: Selected Speeches and Writings.* Chicago: Lawrence Hill Books, 1999.

Fott, David. *John Dewey: America's Philosopher of Democracy.* Lanham, MD: Rowman and Littlefield, 1998.

Franklin, Benjamin. *Autobiography.* 1793; New York: P. F. Collier and Son Company, 2012.

Freud, Sigmund. *Civilization and Its Discontents.* 1941; New York: W. W. Norton and Company, 1989.

Frieden, Terry. "Mississippi Town Sued over 'School-to-Prison Pipeline.'" *CNN.com.* October, 26, 2012. http://www.cnn .com/2012/10/24/justice/mississippi-civil-rights-lawsuit/.

Friedman, Benjamin M. *The Moral Consequences of Economic Growth.* New York: Vintage Books, Random House, 2005.

Friere, Paulo. *Pedagogy of the Oppressed.* London: Continuum International Publishing Group, 2006.

Frost, Jennifer J., and Jacqueline Darroch Forrest. "Understanding the Impact of Effective Teenage Pregnancy Prevention Programs." *Family Planning Perspectives* 27, no. 5 (1995): 188–95.

Fustenberg, François. "Beyond Freedom and Slavery: Autonomy, Virtue, and Resistance in Early American Political Discourse." *Journal of American History* 89, no. 4 (2003): 1295–1330.

Galston, William. "The Perils of Polarization." *New Republic,* April 5, 2010. http://www.tnr.com/blog/william-galston/the -perils-polarization.

Gámez-Gaudix, Manuel, Murray A. Straus, José Antonio Carrobles, Marina J. Muñoz-Rivas, and Carmen Almendros. "Corporal Punishment and Long-Term Behavior Problems: The Moderating Role of Positive Parenting and Psychological Aggression." *Psicothema* 22, no. 5 (2010): 529–36.

Gardner, Howard. *Leading Minds: An Anatomy of Leadership.* New York: Basic Books, 1995.

Gardner, John W. *On Leadership.* New York: The Free Press, 1990.

Gastil, John. "A Definition and Illustration of DemocraticLeadership." *Human Relations* 47, no. 8 (1994): 953–75.

Geiser, Saul, and Maria Veronica Santelices. "Validity of High-School Grades in Predicting Student Success beyond the Freshman Year: High School Record vs. Standardized Tests as Indicators of Four-Year College Outcomes." *U.C. Berkeley Center for Studies in Higher Education, Research and Occasional Paper.* Series 6 (2007): 1–35. http://escholarship.org/uc/item/7306z0zf.

Gencer, Arin. "'Virtues Project' encourages students to find the good in themselves." *Baltimore Sun*, February 4, 2009. http://aacps.org/admin/articlefiles/422-CharacterEducationNewsletterJanuary2011.pdf.

Germain, David. "Morgan Freeman Pays for Integrated Prom in New Documentary." *Huffington Post*, January 16, 2009. http://www.huffingtonpost.com/2009/01/16/morgan-freeman-pays-for-i_n_158628.html.

Gershoff, Elizabeth T., and Susan H. Bitensky. "The Case against Corporal Punishment of Children: Converging Evidence from Social Science Research and International Human Rights Law and Implications for U.S. Public Policy." *Psychology, Public Policy, and Law* 13, no. 4 (2007): 231–72.

Gerson, Michael. "America's Politics of Polarization." *Washington Post*, July 17, 2012, A15.

Ghali, Khalifa H. "Government Spending and Economic Growth in Saudi Arabia." *Journal of Economic Development* 22, no. 2 (1997): 165–72.

Gladwell, Malcolm. *Outliers: The Story of Success.* New York: Bay Back Books, 2011.

Glanz, Karen, and Amy L. Yaroch. "Strategies for Increasing Fruit and Vegetable Intake in Grocery Stores and Communities: Policy, Pricing, and Environmental Change." *Preventive Medicine* 39, Supplement 2 (September 2004): S75-S80.

Gouldner, Alvin W., ed. *Studies in Leadership: Leadership and Democratic Action.* New York: Russell & Russell, 1950.

Grabo, Carl H. "Education for Democratic Leadership." *Journal of Sociology* 23, no. 6 (1918): 763–78.

Greeley, Brendan. "Bernanke to Economists: More Philosophy, Please." *BusinessWeek*, August 6, 2012. http://www.business week.com/articles/2012-08-06/bernanke-to-economists -more-philosphy-please.

Greenberg Quinlan Rosner Research. "Democracy Corps/Campaign for America's Future Poll, Nov, 2008." Retrieved Feb-22-2012 from the iPOLL Databank. The Roper Center for Public Opinion Research. University of Connecticut.

Greenleaf, Robert K., Don M. Frick, and Larry C. Spears, eds. *On Becoming a Servant-Leader.* San Francisco: Jossey-Bass, 1996.

Grier, Kevin B., and Gordun Tullock. "An Empirical Analysis of Cross-National Economic Growth, 1951–1980." *Journal of Monetary Economics* 24, no. 2 (September 1989): 259–76.

Grint, Keith. *The Arts of Leadership.* New York: Oxford University Press, 2001.

———. *Leadership: A Very Short Introduction.* New York: Oxford University Press, 2010.

Grint, Keith, ed. *Leadership: Classical, Contemporary, and Critical Approaches.* New York: Oxford University Press, 1997.

Guo, Gang. "The Timing of the Influences of Cumulative Poverty on Children's Cognitive Ability and Achievement." *Social Forces* 77, no. 1 (1998): 257–87.

Gylfason, Thorvaldur, and Gylfi Zoega. "Natural Resources and Economic Growth: The Role of Investment." *World Economy* 29, no. 8 (2006): 1091–1115.

Hager, Eli. "Still Separate and Unequal." *Washington Post*, May 14, 2012, A13.

Hamilton, Alexander, James Madison, and John Jay. *The Federalist Papers.* Edited by Lawrence Goldman. New York: Oxford University Press, 2008.

Harlow, James G. "Purpose-Defining: The Central Function of

the School Administrator." In *Preparing Administrators: New Perspectives*. Edited by J. A. Culbertson and S. P. Hencley, 61–71. Columbus, OH: University Council for Educational Administration, 1962.

Harper, Maxine. *Maxine Harper's Journey of Hope.* Oxford, MS: Lantern Publishing, 2011.

Harwood, John. "Deep Philosophical Divide Underlies the Impasse." *New York Times*, March 2, 2013, A10.

Hassler, Patti. "Families Struggle: Child Poverty Remains High." *Children's Defense Fund.* September 20, 2012. http://www .childrensdefense.org/newsroom/cdf-in-the-news/press -releases/2012/child-poverty-remains-high.html.

Hebert, Christopher G. "Sentencing Outcomes of Black, Hispanic, and White Males Convicted under Federal Sentencing Guidelines." *Criminal Justice Review* 22, no. 2 (1997): 133–56.

Heller, Joel A. "Fearing Fear Itself: Photo Identification Laws, Fear of Fraud, and the Fundamental Right to Vote." *Vanderbilt Law Review* 62, no. 6 (November 2009): 1871–1912.

Helo, Ari, and Peter Onuf. "Jefferson, Morality, and the Problem of Slavery." *William and Mary Quarterly* 60, no. 3 (July 2003): 583–614.

Herbert, Bob. "The System's Broken." *New York Times*, October 30, 2006, A25.

Herd, Pamela, Brian Goesling, and James S. House. "Socioeconomic Position and Health: The Differential Effects of Education versus Income on the Onset versus Progression of Health Problems." *Journal of Health and Social Behavior* 48 (September 2007): 223–38.

Hickman, Larry. "John Dewey's Spiritual Values." In *Dewey's Enduring Impact: Essays on America's Philosopher*. Edited by John Shook and Paul Kurtz, 193–203. Albany, NY: Prometheus Books, 2011.

———. *Philosophical Tools for Technological Culture: Putting*

Pragmatism to Work. Bloomington: Indiana University Press, 2001.

———. "Socialization, Social Efficiency, and Social Control." In *John Dewey and Our Educational Prospect*. Edited by David T. Hansen, 67–79. Albany, NY: State University of New York Press, 2006.

Hickman, Larry A., gen. ed. *The Correspondence of John Dewey, 1859–1952*. 2nd ed. Edited by Barbara Levine, Anne Sharpe, and Harriet Furst Simon. Charlottesville, VA : InteLex, 2001.

Hill, Jim, and Rand Cheadle. *The Bible Tells Me So: Uses and Abuses of Holy Scripture*. New York: Anchor Books, 1995.

Hill, Marianne T. *Mississippi Economic Review and Outlook* 22, no. 1. Jackson: Mississippi Institutions of Higher Learning, 2008.

Himmelfarb, Dan. "The Constitutional Relevance of the Second Sentence of the Declaration of Independence." *Yale Law Journal* 100, no. 1 (1990): 169–87.

Hobbes, Thomas. *Leviathan*. 1651; New York: Penguin Classics, 1982.

Hochschild, Jennifer L. *Facing Up to the American Dream: Race, Class, and the Soul of the Nation*. Princeton, NJ: Princeton University Press, 1995.

Hoffman, Jan. "Does 8th-Grade Pomp Fit the Circumstance." *New York Times*. June 22, 2008, ST1. http://www.nytimes.com/2008/06/22/fashion/22grad.html.

Hogan, Ron. "Looking at Leadership, Then and Now: *PW* Talks with James MacGregor Burns." *Publishers Weekly* 250, no. 13 (March 31, 2003): 56.

Holy Bible. New King James Version.

Hoogeveen, Johannes G., and Berk Özler. *Not Separate, Not Equal: Poverty and Inequality in Post-Apartheid South Africa*. William Davidson Institute Working Paper 739 (January

2005): 1–41. http://wdi.umich.edu/files/publications/working papers/wp739.pdf.

Hoover-Dempsey, Kathleen V., Joan M. T. Walker, Kathleen P. Jones, and Richard P. Reed. "Teachers Involving Parents (TIP): Results of an In-Service Teacher Education Program for Enhancing Parental Involvement." *Teaching and Teacher Education* 18, no. 7 (October 2002): 843–67.

Horowitz, Alana. "Congress Approval Rating Lower Than Porn, Polygamy, BP Oil Spill, 'U.S. Going Communist.'" *Huffington Post*. November 17, 2011. http://www.huffingtonpost .com/2011/11/16/n_1098497.html.

Hughes, Brendan. "To the Manner Born: The Way Your Birth Order Shapes Your Character." *Western Mail* (Cardiff, UK), February 5, 2011, 14.

Hume, David. *A Treatise on Human Nature*. Edited by L. A. Selby-Bigge. 1738; New York: Oxford University Press, 1990.

Huntley, Helen. "For Floridians, the Tax Burden Is Even Lighter." *St. Petersburg Times*, April 9, 2004, 1A.

Ideas That Work. Washington, DC: Appalachian Regional Commission, 2000.

Jackson, Tim. *Prosperity without Growth: Economics for a Finite Planet*. London: Routledge, 2009.

James, William. "On a Certain Blindness in Human Beings." In *Talks to Teachers on Psychology: And to Students on Some of Life's Ideals*. By William James. 149–69. New York: W. W. Norton, 1958.

———. "The Sentiment of Rationality." In *The Will to Believe and Other Essays in Popular Philosophy*. By William James. New York: Longmans, Green, 1911.

———. "The Social Value of the College-Bred." In *The Works of William James: Essays, Comments, and Reviews*. Edited by Ignas Skrupskelis, 106–12. Cambridge, MA: Harvard University Press, 1987.

Jamieson, Alastair. "Scotland Rejects Independence in Record-Breaking Referendum." *NBC News*, September 18, 2014. http://www.nbcnews.com/storyline/scotland-independence-vote/scotland-rejects-independence-record-breaking-referendum-n206876.

Jefferson, Thomas. "Letter from Thomas Jefferson to Uriah Forrest (Dec. 31, 1787)." In *The Papers of Thomas Jefferson*. Vol. 12. Edited by Julian P. Boyd, 478. Princeton, NJ: Princeton University Press, 1955.

Jemmott, John B., Loretta S. Jemmott, and Geoffrey T. Fong. "Efficacy of a Theory-Based Abstinence-Only Intervention Over 24 Months." *Archives of Pediatric Adolescent Medicine* 164, no. 2 (2010): 152–59.

Johns Hopkins Researchers. "Dropout Factories: Take a Closer Look at Failing Schools Across the Country." *Associated Press*, 2007. http://hosted.ap.org/specials/interactives/wdc/dropout/.

Jones, James H. *Bad Blood: The Tuskegee Syphilis Experiment*. New and expanded ed. New York: The Free Press, 1993.

Jones, Nate. "Want to be Class President in Mississippi? You Need to Be White." *Time*, August 27, 2010. http://newsfeed.time.com/2010/08/27/want-to-be-class-president-in-mississippi-you-need-to-be-white/.

Jones, Royce P. Review of *Morality, Leadership, and Public Policy*. By Eric Thomas Weber. *Journal of Speculative Philosophy* 26, no. 1 (2012): 76–78.

Jonescu, Daren. "The Case against Public Education." *American Thinker*, February 26, 2012. http://www.americanthinker.com/2012/12/the_case_against_public_education.html.

Jossey-Bass Publishers and Michael Fullan. *The Jossey-Bass Reader on Educational Leadership*. 2nd ed. San Francisco: Jossey-Bass of John Wiley and Sons, 2007.

"Judicious." *Dictionary.com*. Collins English Dictionary—Com-

plete and Unabridged. 10th ed. HarperCollins Publishers.
http://dictionary.reference.com/browse/judicious.

"Julius Minor." (Obituary). *Toledo Blade* (OH), September 28,
2012. http://www.legacy.com/obituaries/toledoblade/obituary
.aspx?pid=160149085.

Justice Department. FBI Press Release. *Mississippi Man Pleads
Guilty to Conspiring to Commit Hate Crimes Against African-
Americans in Jackson.* Washington, DC: Justice Department
Documents and Publications, January 3, 2013.

Kandel, I. L. "The Influence of Dewey Abroad." *Teachers College
Record* 31, no. 3 (1929): 239–44.

Kane, John, and Haig Patapan. *The Democratic Leader.* New York:
Oxford University Press, 2012.

———. "The Neglected Problem of Democratic Leadership."
Public Leadership: Perspectives and Practices. Edited by Paul
't Hart and John Uhr, 25–36. Canberra: Australian National
University Press, 2008.

Keen, Judy. "As Winter Moves In, Homeless Live in Cars." *USA
Today*, December 1, 2012, 3A.

Kellerman, Barbara. "Thinking About . . . Leadership—Warts and
All." *Harvard Business Review* 82, no. 1, (2004): 40–45.

Kezar, Adrianna, Tricia Bertram Gallant, and Jaime
Lester."Everyday People Making a Difference on College
Campuses: The Tempered Grassroots Leadership Tactics
of Faculty and Staff." *Studies in Higher Education* 36, no. 2
(March 2011): 129–51.

King, Martin Luther, Jr. *A Testament of Hope: The Essential
Writings and Speeches of Martin Luther King, Jr.* New York:
HarperOne, 1990.

———. *Why We Can't Wait.* New York: Signet Classics, 2000.

King, P. M., and K. S. Kitchener. *Developing Reflective Judgment:
Understanding and Promoting Intellectual Growth and Criti-*

cal *Thinking in Adolescents and Adults*. San Francisco: Jossey-
Bass, 1994.

KIPP Delta Public Schools. "Benchmark Exam: Results." 2010.
http://www.kippdelta.org/academic-results.

"KKK Rally at Ole Miss: Klan Outnumbered by Protestors." *Huffington Post*, March 18, 2010. http://www.huffingtonpost
.com/n_366475.html.

Kohler, Pamela K., Lisa E. Manhart, and William E. Lafferty.
"Abstinence-Only and Comprehensive Sex Education and the
Initiation of Sexual Activity and Teen Pregnancy." *Journal of
Adolescent Health* 42, no. 4 (April 2008): 344–51.

Koopman, Colin. "Pragmatism as a Philosophy of Hope: Emer-
son, James, Dewey, Rorty." *Journal of Speculative Philosophy*
20, no. 2 (2006): 106–16.

Kouzes, James M., and Barry Z. Posner. *The Truth about Leadership: The No-Fads, Heart-of-the-Matter Facts You Need to
Know*. San Francisco: Jossey-Bass, 2010.

Kristof, Nicholas D., and Sheryl WuDunn. "The Women's Crusade." *New York Times Magazine*, August 23, 2009, MM28.
http://www.nytimes.com/2009/08/23/magazine/23Women-t
.html.

Kunda, Gideon. *Engineering Culture: Control and Commitment
in a High Tech Corporation*. Philadelphia: Temple University
Press, 2006.

Kurtz, Paul, and John Shook, eds. *Dewey's Enduring Impact:
Essays on America's Philosopher*. Amherst, NY: Prometheus
Books, 2010.

Kuyper, Jonathan. "Deliberative Democracy and the Neglected
Dimension of Leadership." *Journal of Public Deliberation* 8,
no. 1 (2012): 1–32.

Lachs, John. *A Community of Individuals*. New York: Routledge
Press, 2003.

———. "Stoic Pragmatism." *Journal of Speculative Philosophy* 19, no. 2 (2005): 95–106.

———. *Stoic Pragmatism*. Bloomington: Indiana University Press, 2012.

"leader, n.1." OED Online. September 2012. Oxford University Press (accessed October 5, 2012).

Leadership Statements and Quotes. Department of the Army, Pamphlet 600-65. Washington, DC: Headquarter, Department of the Army, 1985. http://www.au.af.mil/au/awc/awc gate/army/p600_65.pdf.

Lee, Robert E. "Letter to G.W.P. Custis (Jan. 23, 1861)." In *Lee Considered: General Robert E. Lee and Civil War History*. By Alan T. Nolan, 34–35. Chapel Hill: University of North Carolina Press, 1996.

Leichman, Aaron J. "Survey: Nation's 'Most Religious' Population in Mississippi." *Christian Post*, December 22, 2009. http://www.christianpost.com/news/42383/.

Lenkert, Erika. *Frommer's Memorable Walks in San Francisco*. 6th ed. Hoboken, NJ: Wiley, 2006.

Lewin, Kurt. "The Consequences of an Authoritarian and Democratic Leadership." In *Studies in Leadership: Leadership and Democratic Action*. Edited by A. W. Gouldner, 409–17. New York: Russell & Russell, 1950.

Lewin, Kurt, Ronald Lippit, and Ralph K. White. "Patterns of Aggressive Behavior in Experimentally Created 'Social Climates.'" *Journal of Social Psychology, S.P.S.S.I. Bulletin* 10, no. 2 (1939): 271–99.

Locke, John. *Second Treatise of Government*. 1689; Indianapolis, IN: Hackett Publishing, 1997.

Luckett, Dwight J. "Roadmap to Success: Dropout Prevention Plan, 2008–2009." Canton Public School District, 2008. http://www.mde.k12.ms.us/docs/dropout-prevention-and

-compulsory-school-attendance-library/canton-public
-school-district.PDF.

Luhby, Tami. "Mississippi Has Highest Poverty and Lowest Income." *CNN Money*, September 20, 2012. http://money
.cnn.com/2012/09/20/news/economy/income-states-poverty/
index.html.

Luke, Jeffrey S. *Catalytic Leadership: Strategies for an Intercon-
nected World*. San Francisco: Jossey-Bass, 1998.

Lyman, Rick. "In Many Schools, the Paddle Is No Relic." *New
York Times*, September 30, 2006, A1.

Lynch, Robert G. *Rethinking Growth Strategies: How State and
Local Taxes and Services Affect Economic Development*.
Washington, DC: Economic Policy Institute, 2004. http://
epi.3cdn.net/f82246f98a3e3421fd_04m6iiklp.pdf.

Machiavelli, Niccolò. *The Prince*. 1532; New York: Penguin Classics, 2011.

MacLean, Nancy. *Behind the Mask of Chivalry: The Making of
the Second Ku Klux Klan*. New York: Oxford University Press,
1994.

Mankiw, N. Gregory, David Romer, and David N. Weil. "A Contribution to the Empirics of Economic Growth." *Quarterly
Journal of Economics* 107, no. 2 (1992): 407–37.

Mantell, Ruth. "Must Have Job Skills in 2013," *Wall Street Journal*,
November 18, 2012. http://online.wsj.com/article/SB10001424
127887324735104578118902763095818.html.

Martin, Jay. *The Education of John Dewey*. New York: Columbia
University Press, 2002.

Mauer, Marc, and Ryan S. King. "Uneven Justice: State Rates of
Incarceration by Race and Ethnicity." *The Sentencing Project*.
Washington, DC, July 2007, 11. http://www.sentencingproject
.org/doc/publications/rd_stateratesofincbyraceandethnicity
.pdf.

Maxwell, John C. *The 21 Irrefutable Laws of Leadership: Fol-*

low Them and People Will Follow You. 1998; Nashville, TN: Thomas Nelson, 2007.

Maynard, Micheline. "With GE, Toyota, Nissan, Manufacturing Booms in Mississippi." *Forbes*, July 10, 2012. http://www .forbes.com/sites/michelinemaynard/2012/07/10/with-ge -toyota-nissan-manufacturing-booms-in-mississippi/.

McCarthy, Patrick T. *2012 Kids Count Data Book: State Trends in Child Well-Being*. Baltimore: Annie E. Casey Foundation, 2012.

McIntyre, Lee. "Making Philosophy Matter—Or Else." *Chronicle of Higher Education*, December 11, 2011, B9–10.

McKibben, Bill. *Deep Economy: The Wealth of Communities and the Durable Future*. New York: Henry Holt, 2007.

Meadmore, Daphne, and Colin Symes. "Keeping Up Appearances: Uniform Policy for School Diversity?" *British Journal of Educational Studies* 45, no. 2 (1997): 174–86.

———. "Of Uniform Appearance: A Symbol of School Discipline and Governmentality." *Discourse* 17, no. 2 (1996): 209–25.

Mellman, Mark. "Moderate and Polarized." *The Hill*, January 25, 2005. http://thehill.com/opinion/columnists/mark -mellman/8564-moderate-and-polarized.

Meyerson, Harold. "An Ongoing Civil War." *Washington Post*, April 13, 2011, A15.

Michael, Joel A., and Harold I. Modell. *Active Learning in Secondary and College Science Classrooms: A Working Model of Helping the Learning to Learn*. Mahwah, NJ: Erlbaum, 2003.

Mill, John Stuart. *On Liberty*. 1859; Binghamton, NY: Vail-Ballou Press, 2003.

Miller, Julie A. "Delta Dawn." *Education Week*, Supplement: "Quality Counts," 16, no. 17 (1997): 143–45.

Mississippi Center for Education Innovation. "About Us: Planting Seeds . . . Charting Courses." Learning Labs, 2008. http://

www.kellogglearninglabs.org/upload_main/docs/ms-aagd
-web_09-03-19.pdf.

Mississippi Center for Public Policy. "MS High School Graduation Rates, 2010–2011." *MCPP Reports.* 2011. http://
www.mspolicy.org/mcpp_reports/mcpp_reports_view
.php?entryID=334.

"Mississippi Delta Revitalization: Goals and Recommendations
2008." The Special Task Force for the Revitalization of the
Delta Region. http://www.mississippi.edu/drtf/downloads/
delta_task_force_recc_for_2008.pdf.

Mississippi Economic Development Council. "Executive Summary of Momentum Mississippi's 2004 Economic Development
Incentive Legislation Proposal." http://www.msmec.com/in
dex.php/2004-blueprint-mississippi/executive-summary.

Mississippi Economic Policy Center. "The Nuts and Bolts of the
Mississippi Budget: A Taxpayer's Guide to the Mississippi
Budget." Jackson, MS: Hope Enterprise Corporation and the
Mississippi Economic Policy Center, 2012. http://mepconline
.org/images/admin/pdfs/179_26933_2012%20Budget%20&%20
Tax%20WEB.pdf.

"Mississippi Turning: Can People Be Made to Change Their
Minds about the Magnolia State?" *The Economist*, January 4,
2007.

Montesquieu, Charles de Secondat, *The Spirit of the Laws*. Edited
by Anne M. Cohler, Basia Carolyn Miller, and Harold Samuel
Stone. 1748; New York: Cambridge University Press, 1989.

Moore, Malcolm. "Thousands Line Street to Mourn Policeman
Killed in Football Riot." *Daily Telegraph* (London), February 6,
2007, 15.

Mosle, Sara. "Report Card." *New York Times*, August 21, 2011,
BR1.

Mullins, Andrew P. *Building Consensus: A History of the Passage
of the Mississippi Education Reform Act of 1982*. Waynesboro,

MS: The Phil Hardin Foundation and the Mississippi Humanities Council, 1992.

Murphy, Joseph. "Reculturing the Profession of Educational Leadership: New Blueprints." *Yearbook of the National Society for the Study of Education* 101, no. 1 (April 2002): 65–82.

Murray, Mary, Erin Curran, and Denise Zellers. "Building Parent/Professional Partnerships: An Innovative Approach for Teacher Education." *The Teacher Educator* 43, no. 2 (2008): 87–108.

Nave, Ryan L. "Graduation Rates, Test Scores Up." *Jackson Free Press*, August 29, 2012. http://www.jacksonfreepress.com/news/2012/aug/29/graduation-rates-test-score/.

Nhan, Doris. "Analysis: How Much States Spend on Their Kids Really Does Matter." *National Journal*, October 23, 2012. http://www.nationaljournal.com/thenextamerica/education/analysis-how-much-states-spend-on-their-kids-really-does-matter-20121016.

Nicholson, Hunter. "Race and the Greek System at Ole Miss." *Daily Mississippian* (Oxford), September 20, 2011, 2–3.

Niemann, Yolanda Flores. "The Making of a Token: A Case Study of Stereotype Threat, Stigma, Racism, and Tokenism in Academe." *Frontiers: A Journal of Women Studies* 20, no. 1 (1999): 111–34.

Novack, George. *Pragmatism versus Marxism: An Appraisal of John Dewey's Philosophy.* 1975. New York: Pathfinder Press, 2003.

Novak, John M. *Inviting Educational Leadership: Fulfilling Potential and Applying an Ethical Perspective to the Educational Process.* New York: Pearson Education, 2002.

Nozick, Robert. *Anarchy, the State, and Utopia.* New York: Basic Books, 1974.

———. "Why Do Intellectuals Oppose Capitalism? Exce(rpted)." *Cato Policy Report* XX, no. 1 (January–February 1998). http://

www.libertarianism.org/publications/essays/why-do-intellec tuals-oppose-capitalism.

Nye, Joseph S. *The Powers to Lead*. New York: Oxford University Press, 2008.

Nye, Joseph S., Philip Zelikow, and David King, eds. *Why People Don't Trust Government*. Cambridge, MA: Harvard University Press, 1997.

Okruhlik, Gwenn. "Networks of Dissent: Islamism and Reform in Saudi Arabia." *Current History* 101, no. 651 (2002): 22–28.

Omran, Mohammed, and Ali Bolbol. "Foreign Direct Investment, Financial Development, and Economic Growth: Evidence from the Arab Countries." *Review of Middle East Economics and Finance* 1, no. 3 (2003): 231–49.

Oreopoulos, Philip. "Do Dropouts Drop Out Too Soon? Wealth, Health, and Happiness from Compulsory Schooling." *Journal of Public Economics* 91, nos. 11–12, (December 2007): 2213–229.

Orfield, Gary. "Schools More Separate: Consequences of a Decade of Resegregation." *Harvard Civil Rights Project*. Cambridge, MA: Harvard University, 2001, 1–55. http://www.eric .ed.gov/PDFS/ED459217.pdf.

Ornstein, Norman J. "Reagan Was a Master of the Art of Compromise." *New York Times*, November 13, 2012. http://www .nytimes.com/roomfordebate/2012/06/11/could-ronald-rea gan-lead-todays-gop/reagan-was-a-master-of-the-art-of -compromise.

Parrish, John. "Who Wants to Rule the World? Are You Born with Leadership Skills? Or Can They Be Taught?" *Evening Standard* (London), September 28, 1998, 7.

Passow, A. Harry. "John Dewey's Influence on Education around the World." *Teachers College Record* 83, no. 3 (1982): 401–18.

Pender, Geoff. "GOP Split on Charter Bills." *Clarion Ledger* (Jackson, MS), January 24, 2013, 1A-2A.

Peterson, Andrew. "Mississippi Manufacturing: Toyota Completing Mississippi Plant for Corolla." *Motor Trend*, June 17, 2010. http://wot.motortrend.com/mississippi-manufacturing-toyota-completing-mississippi-plant-for-corolla-8985.html.

Pilkington, Ed. "United States: Black Couple's Wedding Ruined by Churchgoers." *The Guardian* (London), July 30, 2012, 14.

Pinkerton, Jim. "Rising Tide for the American People: Prosperity Goes Up as Corporate Tax Goes Down." *Washington Times*, December 9, 2011, B1.

Plato. "Apology." In *The Collected Dialogues of Plato*. Edited by Edith Hamilton and Huntington Cairns. Princeton, NJ: Princeton University Press, 1996.

———. "Apology." In *Five Dialogues*. Translated by G. M. A. Grube. Edited by John M. Cooper. Indianapolis, IN: Hackett Publishing, 2002.

———. "Meno." In *The Collected Dialogues of Plato*. Edited by Edith Hamilton and Huntington Cairns. Princeton, NJ: Princeton University Press, 1996.

———. "Phaedo." In *The Collected Dialogues of Plato*. Edited by Edith Hamilton and Huntington Cairns. Princeton, NJ: Princeton University Press, 1996.

———. *The Republic*. Translated by G. M. A. Grube. Indianapolis, IN: Hackett Publishing, 1992.

Pojman, Louis, and Robert Westmoreland. *Equality: Selected Readings*. New York: Oxford University Press, 1997.

Pomerantz, Gary M. *Where Peachtree Meets Sweet Auburn: A Saga of Race and Family*. New York: Penguin Books, 1996.

Powell, Jonathan. *The New Machiavelli: How to Wield Power in the Modern World*. New York: Random House, 2012.

Price, Terry L. *Leadership Ethics: An Introduction*. New York: Cambridge University Press, 2008.

———. *Understanding Ethical Failures in Leadership*. New York: Cambridge University Press, 2006.

Pritchard, Michael. "Philosophy for Children." *Stanford Encyclopedia of Philosophy*. Summer 2009 ed. Edited by Edward N. Zalta. http://plato.stanford.edu/archives/sum2009/entries/children/.

Putnam, Robert. "Bowling Alone: America's Declining Social Capital." *Journal of Democracy* 6, no. 1 (1995): 65–78.

Raico, Ralph. *Great Wars and Great Leaders: A Libertarian Rebuttal*. Auburn, AL: Ludwig von Mises Institute, 2010.

Ralston, Shane. *John Dewey's Great Debates–Reconstructed*. Charlotte, NC: Information Age, 2011.

Rawls, John. *Political Liberalism*. New York: Columbia University Press, 1996.

———. *A Theory of Justice*. Cambridge, MA: Harvard University Press, 1999.

Reilly, Mollie. "Chris McDaniel Accuses GOP of 'Abandoning the Conservative Movement' after Runoff Loss." *Huffington Post*, June 25, 2014. http://www.huffingtonpost.com/2014/06/25/chris-mcdaniel-republicans_n_5528041.html.

Reynolds, Alan. "Lower Tax Rates Mean Faster Economic Growth." *Creators.com*, November 14, 2002. http://www.cato.org/publications/commentary/lower-tax-rates-mean-faster-economic-growth.

Riley, Kathryn. "'Democratic Leadership'—A Contradiction in Terms?" *Leadership and Policy in Schools* 2, no. 2 (2003): 125–40.

Rogers, Melvin. *The Undiscovered Dewey*. New York: Columbia University Press, 2009.

Romano, Carlin. *America the Philosophical*. New York: Knopf, 2012.

Rose, Mike. *The Mind at Work: Valuing the Intelligence of the American Worker*. New York: Penguin Books, 2005.

Rossell, Christine H. "School Desegregation and White Flight."

Political Science Quarterly 90, no. 4 (Winter 1975–1976): 675–95.

Rost, Joseph C. *Leadership for the Twenty-First Century*. Westport, CT: Praeger, 1993.

Ruscio, Kenneth P. *The Leadership Dilemma in Modern Democracy*. Northampton, MA: Edward Elgar Publishing, 2004.

Russell, Bertrand. *Religion and Science*. 1935; New York: Oxford University Press, 1997.

Ryff, Carol D., and Burton H. Singer. "Know Thyself and Become What You Are: A Eudaomonic Approach to Psychological Well-Being." *Journal of Happiness Studies* 9 (2008): 13–39.

Sachs, Jeffrey D. *Common Wealth: Economics for a Crowded Planet*. New York: Penguin Press, 2008.

Salter, Sid. "Charter Schools Offer Alternative to Mediocre/Failing Schools." *Desoto Times Tribune* (MS), February 22, 2012. http://www.desototimes.com/articles/2012/02/23/opinion/editorials/doc4f453f741ac69454084633.txt.

Sandel, Michael J. *Public Philosophy: Essays on Morality in Politics*. Cambridge, MA: Harvard University Press, 2006.

Sauter, Michael B., Samuel Weigley, Alexander E. M. Hess, and Brian Zajac. "States with the Highest (and Lowest) Taxes." *24/7 Wall St.*, October 23, 2012. http://247wallst.com/2012/10/23/states-where-residents-pay-the-most-in-taxes/.

Schein, Edgar H. *Organizational Culture and Leadership*. San Francisco: Jossey-Bass, 2010.

Schroeder, Elizabeth. *Comprehensive Sex Ed the Most Effective Approach to Reducing STDs and Pregnancy, Rutgers Experts Say*. Rutgers News Release, February 3, 2010. http://news.rutgers.edu/medrel/news-releases/2010/01/comprehensive-sex-ed-20100203.

Seneca, Lucius Annaeus. *Letters from a Stoic*. New York: Penguin Classics, 1969.

Sergiovanni, T. J. *The Principalship: A Reflective Practice Perspective*. 2nd ed. Boston: Allyn & Bacon, 1991.

Severson, Kim. "Mississippi Tells Public Schools to Develop Policies Allowing Prayers." *New York Times*, March 16, 2013, A13.

Shook, John Robert, and Paul Kurtz, eds. *Dewey's Enduring Impact: Essays on America's Philosopher*. Amherst, NY: Prometheus Books, 2010.

Shirley, Scott. "For Students, 'Zip Code Does Not Define Destiny.'" *Take Part*, November 28, 2012. http://www.takepart.com/article/2012/11/28/kipp-delta-zip-code-not-define-destiny.

Sigo, Shelly. "Mississippi: Gov. Oks $3.5b for Schools." *The Bond Buyer*, May 2, 2007.

Silver, James W. *Mississippi: The Closed Society*. 1964; Jackson: University of Mississippi Press, 2012.

Smith, Thomas Vernor. "Democratic Leadership." *Scientific Monthly* 21, no. 6 (December 1925): 613–28.

Smrekar, Claire, James W. Guthrie, Debra E. Owens, and Pearl G. Sims. *March toward Excellence: School Success and Minority Student Achievement in Department of Defense Schools*. Washington, DC: National Education Goals Panel, September 2001. http://govinfo.library.unt.edu/negp/reports/DoDFinal921.pdf.

SouthernEcho. "Mississippi School Districts Corporal Punishment Incidents: 2009–2010 to 2010–2011 School Years." 2012. http://southernecho.org/s/wp-content/uploads/2012/01/01-12-12-map-ms-sch-dist-corp-punshmnt-change-09-10-to-10-11-v7.pdf

Sperling, Gene. "Rising-Tide Economics." *Democracy: A Journal of Ideas* 6 (Fall 2007): 61–73.

Stackhouse, John. "Pilgrims Meet Death at Hindu Shrines: Sixty Die in Stampedes at Temple." *Globe and Mail* (Toronto), July 16, 1996, A1.

Starkey, Ken. "Academic View: A New Philosophy of Leadership."

The Economist, February 9, 2012. http://www.economist.com/
whichmba/academic-view-new-philosophy-leadership.

Starratt, Robert J. "Democratic Leadership Theory in Late Modernity: An Oxymoron or Ironic Possibility?" *International Journal of Leadership in Education* 4, no. 4 (2001): 333–52.

———. "Democratic Leadership Theory in Late Modernity: An Oxymoron or Ironic Possibility." In *The Ethical Dimensions of School Leadership*. Edited by Paul T. Begley and Olof Johansson, 13–31. Dordrecht, The Netherlands: Kluwer Academic Publishers, 2003.

Straus, Murray A. "Criminogenic Effects of Corporal Punishment by Parents." In *Transational Criminology Manual*. Vol. I. Edited by M. Herzog-Evans and Isabelle Dréan-Rivette, 373–90. Amsterdam: Wolf Legal Publishing, 2010.

Straus, Murray A., and Emily M. Douglas. "Research on Spanking by Parents: Implications for Public Policy." *Family Psychologist: Bulletin of the Division of Family Psychology* 43, no. 24 (2008): 18–20.

Strauss, Leo. "On Plato's Republic." In *The City and Man*. By Leo Strauss. Chicago: University of Chicago Press, 1978.

Stringfellow, Thornton. *Scriptural and Statistical Views in Favor of Slavery*. Richmond, VA: J. W. Randolph, 1865.

Subedi, Madhusudan. "Caste System: Theories and Practices in Nepal." *Himalayan Journal of Sociology and Anthropology* IV (2010): 134–59.

Taylor, Ephren. *Creating Success from the Inside Out*. Hoboken, NJ: Wiley, 2008.

Thaler, Richard, and Cass Sunstein. *Nudge: Improving Decisions about Health, Wealth, and Happiness*. New York: Penguin Books, 2009.

Thoman, Lexi. "The Ghosts of Ole Miss Are Far from Dead." *Daily Mississippian*. November 8, 2012, 3. http://archive.thed monline.com/article/ghosts-ole-miss-arc-far-dead.

Thomas, Oliver. "A Poverty, Not Education, Is Crisis in U.S.A."
USA Today, December 11, 2013, 8A.

"The UM / 2020 Strategic Plan." *University of Mississippi*, 2012.
http://www.olemiss.edu/um2020/UM2020Report.pdf.

US Census Bureau. "Profile of General Population and Housing
Characteristics: 2010." *2010 Demographic Profile Data*, 2011.
http://factfinder2.census.gov/faces/tableservices/jsf/pages/
productview.xhtml?src=bkmk.

Vedder, Richard, and Bryan O'Keefe. "Wal-Mart against the
Wall?" *Washington Times*, August 27, 2006, B04.

Watkins, Brittany. "Rural, Poor, Successful: Every Arkansas KIPP
Delta Grad Accepted into College." *Clarion Ledger* (Jackson,
MS), February 16, 2013. http://www.clarionledger.com/ar
ticle/20130217/OPINION03/302170002/.

Weber, Eric Thomas. "Choosing Civility: The Lemonade Lesson."
Clarion Ledger (Jackson, MS). September 19, 2010, 8-9B.

———. "Cultural Divides: Barriers Remain to Educational Attainment." *Clarion Ledger* (Jackson, MS). June 6, 2010, C1–2.

———. *Democracy and Leadership: On Pragmatism and Virtue.*
Lanham, MD: Lexington Books, 2013.

———. "Democratic Political Leadership." Chapter 13 in *Political
and Civic Leadership: A Reference Handbook.* Edited by Richard A. Couto, 105–110. Thousand Oaks, CA: SAGE Publications, 2010.

———. "Deweyan Experimentalism and Leadership." Chapter 19
in *Dewey's Enduring Impact: Essays on America's Philosopher.*
Edited by John Robert Shook and Paul Kurtz, 293–301. Amherst, NY: Prometheus Books, 2010.

———. "Greening Industry and Green Industries in Mississippi."
ProBizMS.com., April 8, 2012. https://www.academia
.edu/3000337/Greening_Industry_And_Green_Industries_
In_MS.

———. "A Historical Mandate for Expanding Broadband Internet

Infrastructure." *Review of Policy Research* 27, no. 5 (September 2010): 681–89.

———. "James, Dewey, and Democracy," *William James Studies* 4, no. 1 (December 2009): 90–110.

———. "Learning from Others: What South Korean Technology Policy Can Teach Mississippi." *Review of Policy Research* 25, no. 6 (December 2008): 608–613.

———. "Lessons for Leadership from Keping and Dewey." *Skepsis* 19, nos. 1, 2 (2008): 100–11.

———. "Liberty, Health Care Reform Fit." *Clarion Ledger* (Jackson, MS), January 30, 2011, 13B.

———. "Mississippians Are Ready for Comprehensive Sex Education." *Science Progress*, February 14, 2012. http://scien ceprogress.org/2012/02/mississippians-are-ready-for-compre hensive-sex-education/.

———. *Morality, Leadership, and Public Policy: On Experimental- ism in Ethics.* London: Continuum International Publishing Group, 2011.

———. "On Applying Ethics: Who's Afraid of Plato's Cave?" *Con- temporary Pragmatism* 7, no. 2 (December 2010): 91–103.

———. "Rand's Appeal Curious." *Clarion Ledger* (Jackson, MS). July 24, 2011, C1–2.

———. *Rawls, Dewey, and Constructivism.* London: Continuum International Publishing Group, 2010.

———. "Religious Reasons against Initiative 26." *Oxford Eagle* (Oxford, MS), October 24, 2011, 4A.

———. "Teachers Offer Hope for Mississippi." *Clarion Ledger* (Jackson, MS). April 8, 2012, C1–2.

———. "Try Charter Schools Experiment Where Others Failing." *Clarion Ledger* (Jackson, MS), March 6, 2010, A9. http://www .clarionledger.com/article/20100306/OPINION/3060305/.

———. "Violence Taught when Corporal Punishment Used." *Clarion Ledger* (Jackson, MS), May 14, 2013, 9. https://www

.academia.edu/3533946/_Violence_Taught_when_Corporal_Punishment_Used.

Weitz, Betty A. "Equality and Justice in Education: Dewey and Rawls." *Human Studies* 16, no. 4 (1993): 421–34.

West, Cornel. *Democracy Matters: Winning the Fight against Imperialism*. New York: Penguin Books, 2005.

———. *Hope on a Tightrope*. New York: Smiley Books, 2008.

———. "Interview with Tavis Smiley: On Courage." In *Hope on a Tightrope*. CD accompanying the book. New York: Smiley Books, 2008.

———. *Prophecy Deliverance! An Afro-American Revolutionary Christianity*. Philadelphia: Westminster Press, 1982.

West, Phil. "Mississippi Governor Zooms in on Education during State of the State Speech." *Commercial Appeal* (Memphis), January 22, 2013. http://www.commercialappeal.com/news/2013/jan/22/mississippi-governor-zooms-in-education-state/.

Westbrook, Robert B. *John Dewey and American Democracy*. Ithaca, NY: Cornell University Press, 1991.

Westmoreland, William. "Leadership Statements and Quotes." In *Department of the Army, Pamphlet 600-65*. Washington, DC: Headquarter, Department of the Army, 1985. http://www.au.af.mil/au/awc/awcgate/army/p600_65.pdf.

Whoriskey, Peter. "By the Mississippi Delta, a Whole School Left Behind." *Washington Post*, October 28, 2007, A03.

———. "Evangelical Democrat Stirs the Pot in Miss." *Washington Post*, November 5, 2007, A3.

Will, George F. "Ed Schools vs. Education." *Newsweek*, January 16, 2006, 98.

Wilson, James Q. "Against the Legalization of Drugs." *Commentary*, February 1990. http://www.commentarymagazine.com/article/against-the-legalization-of-drugs/.

Winter, William. "About Us: Planting Seeds . . . Charting Courses." Mississippi Center for Education Innovation, Learning Labs. 2008. http://www.kellogglearninglabs.org/upload_main/docs/ms-aagd-web_09-03-19.pdf (accessed January 26, 2013).

William Winter Institute for Racial Reconciliation. Facebook page, October 15, 2014. https://www.facebook.com/pages/William-Winter-Institute-for-Racial-Reconciliation/295860466710.

Wolf, Susan, and Mira Browne. *Charter Schools in Arizona Perform Significantly below Their Traditional Public School Peers.* Sanford Report Press Release, June 15, 2009. http://credo.stanford.edu/reports/statepressreleases/Arizona.pdf.

Wolfgang, Ben. "Scores Show Students Aren't Ready for College." *Washington Times*, August 17, 2011, A1. http://www.washingtontimes.com/news/2011/aug/17/scores-show-students-not-ready-college/.

Woods, Philip A. "Democratic Leadership: Drawing Distinctions with Distributed Leadership." *International Journal of Leadership in Education* 7, no. 1 (2004): 3–26.

Wren, J. Thomas. *Inventing Leadership: The Challenge of Democracy.* Cheltenham, UK: Edward Elgar Publishing, 2008.

Zakaria, Fareed. "Broken Bootstraps" or (online) "The Downward Path of Upward Mobility." *Washington Post*, November 10, 2011, A25. http://www.washingtonpost.com/gIQAegpS6M_story.html.

Zelizer, Gerald L. "Where Did We Come From? (And What Can We Teach Our Kids?)." *USA Today*, February 7, 2005, 15A.

INDEX